Praise for *The One*

"The future of a habitable plan~~et~~ quo. Inertia and time are unified against us. Laurence Overmire has written a direct, simple, and compelling call to conscience. I hope people hear it."
Aaron Viles, Deputy Director, Gulf Restoration Network

"Overmire takes a stark, uncompromising look at the fractured state of our world today. He pins the cause of our collective predicament on greed, hatred, and delusion and illustrates how our many institutions have succumbed to what the Buddha called the three fires... This is The One Idea that will extinguish the fire, and Overmire offers an array of examples of how to go about the task."
Paul Gerhards, author, *Mapping the Dharma: A Concise Guide to the Middle Way of the Buddha*

"*One Idea* is a wise concept of how we, as individuals, can rise to the enormous challenges we face. It is a roadmap of what we need to do to educate ourselves about these issues and how to take action to fix them. This is a must read for everyone."
Adele Douglass, Founder and Executive Director, Humane Farm Animal Care

"Mark Twain famously said 'Everyone complains about the weather, but no one does anything about it.' Most of us here in America today are somewhat adept at complaining about the disease of the body politic, but very few of us endeavor to do anything about it. Laurence Overmire is doing something about it. The One Idea is a simple, elegant and universally familiar concept that may well be the most potent prescription for what ails our society."
Jeff Farias, musician and radio host

"*The One Idea That Saves The World* is a call for action and a call for unity at a time when our political reality needs it most. Overmire is frank and unflinching in his assessment of the source of our cultural and political division and the ramifications if such division persists. He delivers a sober message on the collective state of human governance in prose, poetry and narrative familiar to us all. But despite all this, Overmire succeeds in ultimately providing a vision of hope and a promise that our efforts in coming together for the benefit of all humankind will be rewarded."
Jessica Pieklo, attorney & writer covering constitutional law and women's rights at Care2.com

"*The One Idea That Saves the World* woke me up like an alarm clock with no snooze button. Once awakened I found a guide and a friend in Laurence Overmire who invited me to consider what's going on in our world and then strengthened me to stay or to become more engaged in taking concrete steps to help make our life together as human beings and our planet better than when I found it. I'm on board and I invite you to join me."
Rev. Jim Smucker, retired, Presbyterian Church (U.S.A.), Lorain, Ohio

"Many people are aware of the shift happening around us. Something is different. The hate, anger, greed, and narcissism we have wallowed in for decades can no longer be ignored. It is time for change... The book is packed with truth, wisdom, and ideas on how to become involved, along with Overmire's inspiring poetry. It challenges us to be our very best selves and be a part of the change. To help you in that goal, I suggest you take along a copy of *The One Idea that Saves the World*."

Jean Sheldon, author, *Monet's Palette*

"Once in a great while a book comes along that contains all the ingredients needed to explain everything important in your life you know to be true but simply never came to you as a single idea that expressed the desires you always had to understand the meaning of life. *The One Idea That Saves The World* is such a book! It is an outline of what Hope looks like... A jewel of a little book to treasure and read over and over again until you cannot help but share its message. An absolute must read!"

Vance Carruth, author, photographer, educator, environmentalist

"It is an uplifting and moving piece... The whole book was very thoughtful and inspiring to me."

Marti Carver, animal rights advocate and caregiver, Dahlonega, Georgia

"*The One Idea* is a strong reminder of what is needed right now to allow human consciousness to emerge and evolve to support life for all... a call to action before it is too late!"

Scott Campbell, Yoga Instructor, Carrboro, North Carolina

"A clear and concise guide to navigating out of our current societal ills, *The One Idea* proves that a better and saner world is within our grasp if only we so choose. There are no promises that it will be easy, but if we all were to simply acknowledge and act upon the self-evident truths espoused in Overmire's book, change would not only be possible, it would be inevitable."

TK Conrad, Information Technology Consultant

"Overmire points to the need for 'immediate personal action' by each and every individual... The book will energize those who comprehend the challenges we are facing, and hopefully awaken others who are not yet aware, are afraid to take action, or think it is someone else's problem."

Marcia G. Yerman, writer, artist, activist, co-founder of cultureID

"This is an urgent message for today, a dream and vision grounded in pressing realities. These realities demand that individuals reconsider who we are and choose to become part of our greater oneness, a new power that will take on the urgent task of saving ourselves and our planet for the future."

Timothy Collins, Assistant Director, Illinois Institute for Rural Affairs and Correspondent, Daily Yonder

"The world has been waiting far too long for this incredible book... There is hope here. There is rational thought. Overmire's intelligent perspective cannot be ignored."

Carol Grier, author, *Choices: a Memoir*

"In a divided world, *The One Idea* is the common ground that allows us to come together to heal and to build a better world despite our differences."

Israa Hasani, counselor in the Intercultural Psychiatric Program, Oregon Health & Science University (OHSU)

"Laurence Overmire has written a book focused on unifying principles and universal truths. He bravely calls out those things that divide us, and challenges readers to act conscientiously. In the tradition of Aldo Leopold, he argues for an ethic of compassion that encompasses all life and the Earth. This book is a beacon of hope and will remain near at hand on my desk to be re-read whenever I am disheartened or feeling small and futile."

Carol Lee-Roark, Ph.D., Hyalite Environmental, LLP

"*The One Idea That Saves The World* is, not surprisingly, both incredibly simple and incredibly profound. It takes a poet to present profound simplicity in language that touches the rhythms of the heart. That poet is Laurence Overmire, and his poetic message is to us a Call to Conscience and a Call to Action, one that will resonate with all the peoples and the rhythms of the planet."

John Lundin, author, *The New Mandala: Eastern Wisdom for Western Living*, written with the Dalai Lama; and *Journey To The Heart Of The World*, written with the indigenous peoples of Colombia

"Clear, focused and spot on. The mission of becoming healthy, as a world, is not as daunting a task when looked at from this most profoundly focused point of view. Especially when one is given the inspiration to make the change happen! I think that when one embraces the purity of The One Idea that a sort of epiphany will happen, as it sends a signal to the soul to open up and let the light out."

Marc J. Rose, Sound Designer, MJR Soundesign Inc.

"At a time when so many have surrendered to cynicism or despair, Overmire throws us a life ring. Drawing upon the wisdom of all ages, his One Idea challenges us to find our collective strength to save life as we know it. This book is fun and easy to read for a wide array of ages, making it a great conversation-starter. I can't wait to buy copies for my two sons!"

Rev. Kate Lore, Minister of Social Justice, First Unitarian Church of Portland, Oregon

"A resounding call to consciousness, a revolution in words – Laurence Overmire boldly rattles the modern penitentiaries of hypocrisy and apathy with this manifesto for global human perseverance by way of love and understanding."

Chad Coenson, author, *Me and Bobby McGee*

"*The One Idea* is a return to common sense and an appeal to the internal goodness we try so hard to ignore in ourselves. In simple language, Overmire reminds us of what we already know: the hour is late, our world is dying, and we are the only ones who can save it. The question is, what will you do with this knowledge?"

Beth Buczynski, writer, Care2

"The One Idea cuts across all the usual divides of politics, religion, nationality, etc. and clearly outlines the challenges to our world that we can all agree on, because they challenge us each on the same level, as a human being. Laurence Overmire reaches the reader through both their heart and their common sense and inspires them to embrace their unique ability to engage in the solution of the challenges we all face, together."

Julia Guthrie, TheUnpluggedLife.com

"The writing is excellent and the quotes woven through the book strongly reinforce the main points. The book has made me think and re-evaluate decisions I have made; the message is getting inside my head and soul. I am accepting that I need to stay involved and take responsibility to keep changes happening."

Paul J. Lyons, Strategic Consultant at Lyons Consulting, LLC

"A cri de Coeur that is both intimate and profound. *The One Idea* challenges us all to examine our own attitude about our responsibility as World Citizens and to take that responsibility to heart at this critical juncture. This Idea unites us through our head, our heart and our spirit."

Marsha Warner, Director of Recruiting, Senior Professional in Human Resources (SPHR)

"This is without a doubt the most important, honest, humble piece of prose and poetry you could read this year. Reading it isn't enough, however. You must be it, live it, do it!"

Donna Marie Miller Ellington, Americans for Healthcare, Too

"Laurence isn't just crying 'fire!' He's providing hope—and practical solutions—for our very survival. A compelling book that I urge everyone on the planet to read. We're all in this together."

Lynn Hasselberger, Founder of myEARTH360.com, Social Media/Marketing Consultant and Editor of elephantjournal.com

"*The One Idea* was quite a ride, from the thoroughly disheartening (but necessary) delineation of the problems we face to proposed solutions that seem so near, so reachable that it gives a cynic hope for humanity's future. After reading *The One Idea*, I'm absolutely certain that the world would be much better off if we had fewer lawyers and more poets running things."

Vincent Reynolds, musician, Shaken Awake

THE ONE IDEA
THAT SAVES THE WORLD

A Call to Conscience and A Call to Action

Laurence Overmire

To John,

Laurence Overmire

4/21/13

INDELIBLE MARK PUBLISHING

Front cover photo: NASA/NOAA/GSFC/Suomi NPP/VIIRS/Norman Kuring

Editing, cover/interior design, author photo: Nancy McDonald

Library of Congress Control Number: 2012936192

ISBN 978-0-9795398-4-8

The quotes of Martin Luther King Jr. and Coretta Scott King -
Reprinted by arrangement with The Heirs to the Estate of Martin Luther King Jr., c/o Writers House as agent for the proprietor New York, NY.
Copyright 1963 Dr. Martin Luther King Jr; copyright renewed 1991 Coretta Scott King

Lawrence, Kushner, *I'm God; You're Not: Observations on Organized Religion & Other Disguises of the Ego*, Jewish Lights Publishing, www.jewishlights.com, Woodstock, VT. Reprinted with permission from the publisher.

David Suzuki & Dave Robert Taylor, *The Big Picture: Reflections on Science, Humanity, and a Quickly Changing Planet,* published by Greystone Books in partnership with the David Suzuki Foundation, 2009. Reprinted with permission from the author.

 INDELIBLE MARK PUBLISHING, LLC
6498 Lowry Drive, # 4
West Linn, OR 97068
www.indeliblemarkpublishing.com
www.imarkbooks.com

Dedicated to
those who do their part every day
to make this world a better place

Also by Laurence Overmire

BOOKS

Honor & Remembrance
A Poetic Journey through American History

Report From X-Star 10
Sci-Fi Poetry

One Immigrant's Legacy
The Overmyer Family in America, 1751-2009

Gone Hollywood

VIDEOPOEMS
View on YouTube

Ode to an Endangered Species

Viewpoint

Beach Walk at Sunset

Maybe the Trees

Visit the author at:

www.laurenceovermire.com

facebook.com/poet.laurence.overmire

CONTENTS

CHAPTER ONE

The House
is on Fire

CHAPTER ONE

The House is on Fire

The people in the house are
Sleeping and in great danger

Seven of their neighbors will come along
Each with an opportunity to save them

Person #1
Does not see the fire
Consumed in his own thoughts
He passes by in ignorant oblivion

Person #2
Sees the fire
But, not wanting to get involved
Walks on by

Person #3
Sees the fire
But, shocked and terrified
Is left immobilized in a state of panic

Person #4
Sees the fire
And immediately takes action
First, phoning the fire department
Then, knocking on the door to
Wake up the inhabitants

Person #5
Sees the fire
And, daring what no one else would
Enters the house to try to
Save the inhabitants

Person #6
Sees the fire
Surveys the scene
And discovers an opportunity
To promote his own interests and
Make a buck
(He's the one handing out
His business card to sell his stuff)

Person #7
Set the fire
And lurks unnoticed
Watching the destruction
Not caring really
About anything at all.

The house is Mother Earth.

Which person are you?

This poem encapsulates the central, overriding issue of our time: our world is on fire and on the verge of collapse; what are each of us willing to do about it? How do we galvanize people to do what is necessary and right?

THE GOOD PEOPLE OF THIS EARTH

"I still believe, in spite of everything, that people are truly good at heart." ~ Anne Frank[1]

I believe in humanity. I believe, like Anne Frank, a young girl with so much promise who ultimately died at the hands of the Nazis in World War II, that despite all the evil we see in the world, most people are indeed truly good at heart. This is what gives me hope.

Of course, we all have our failings and resort to mean-spirited behaviors now and then. All human beings are capable of both good and evil. We all do good things and things that are not so good. We can all be petty, mean, rude, insensitive, and aggressive. But we can also be kind, generous, loving and forgiving. Few would intentionally do serious harm to others.

I disagree with those who believe human beings are inherently wicked or evil. Have you ever seen an evil child? I haven't. I do a lot of teaching in the schools. I've interacted with thousands of kids and I've never seen an evil kindergartner, or first or second or third grader. There might be some kids who have some issues, and most kids do mean things now and then, as we all do, but they're certainly not evil.

All I've ever seen in a tiny, newborn face is innocence, light, and promise. So what is it that we do in our collective dysfunction that takes that which is so positive and good and twists it into something much less?

> *"The potential for humanity lives inside every infant, but healthy development is an effort, not a given. If we do not shelter that spark, guide and nurture it, then we not only lost the life within but we unleash the later destruction on ourselves."*
> ~ Thomas Lewis, et al., *A General Theory of Love*[2]

Every child comes into this world as a gift to humanity. It is up to us, as adults, to see that they are properly taken care of and given all the love and attention they deserve. If we did so, I have no doubt our world would be drastically different and much more humane.

> *"The fact is that people are good. Give people affection and security, and they will give affection and be secure in their feelings and their behavior."* ~ Abraham Maslow

In times of trouble good people come together. I saw this firsthand in the aftermath of the 1994 Northridge earthquake in California. I was

THE HOUSE IS ON FIRE

living in the Hollywood Hills at the time. The quake was devastating in our neighborhood. Two of the houses across the street plunged down the hillside. Neighbors who barely knew each other suddenly came to one another's aid, coordinating their efforts to protect one another, and risking their lives while trying to locate those who were trapped in the rubble.

"Each one of us has the capacity to become a saint. Incredible."
~ Archbishop Desmond Tutu[3]

WHO AM I?

I'm a poet. An actor. An educator. A genealogist. I'm no saint. I'm no guru. I'm far from perfect. I am the so-called "little guy." The guy who struggles to make a living. I am in no way privileged or part of any elite. No corporation pays me to say what I say. I say what I think, what I believe to be the truth.

I'm just a guy trying to make sense of the world. I'm a curious guy. I love learning and I try very hard to know and understand what's going on around me. That's what artists do. They make us more aware. They make us see things, perhaps, from a different angle. As a poet and a genealogist, I tend to see things from a broad, historical perspective, taking into account the Big Picture and the impact on future generations.

This book is a warning and a call to conscience.

I'm disturbed by what I see going on today. Humanity seems to be regressing, not progressing. People are attacking one another over race, religion, class, and culture. Hate and ignorance are becoming fashionable. Good faith, reason and science are all being maligned. Selfishness and greed are being promoted over human decency and the common good.

"Bigotry has become a commonplace of political life in the United States. The jargon of prejudice, sometimes veiled and sometimes

not, is now so prevalent that most people simply shrug their shoulders." ~ Stephen Eric Bronner, Distinguished Professor of Political Science[4]

In American culture, in our politics, we've been cynically divided into the Red Team and the Blue Team. We're all playing football against one another and betting on horse races in the news, but we're not really talking to one another and, most importantly, we are not addressing the dire issues that threaten to destroy human civilization.

I have something to say about this. Hopefully, it is something that will make people stop and think, something that may persuade them to take positive action, to become the 4's or 5's in the poem *The House is on Fire* at the beginning of this chapter.

You see I've been looking for a long time for something that will bridge the differences, something that will overcome the hatred and the violence, something we all have in common that can bring us together to solve the very serious challenges that await us in the coming years. I think I've found something – an idea upon which most people can agree, no matter what their background, culture or religion. It's an old idea, an idea that most of us have pushed aside without really considering its ramifications. It is an idea that is common to all the major religions, an idea that all good people of faith and no faith can support. It is the foundation of all ethics and morality. It has become, I believe, at this crucial juncture in human history, the One Idea that can save the world.

WHO ARE YOU?

That is the big question after all, isn't it? Who are you and what do you believe in? What are you willing to do to save the world? I'm going to ask you to take an honest look at yourself in the course of these few pages. Are you part of the solution or part of the problem? Are you one of those people, the 4's and 5's, who are actively working to put out the fire? These are the heroes, after all, the people who work hard every day in positive ways, large and small, to make this world a better place. These are the people we all respect. These are the people we admire.

These are the leaders who will guide us to a better future. And some of them, those number 5's, are even willing to risk their lives. They charge into the burning house when no one else will. Many have given their lives for our sakes. You know who they are. Some are famous. Some are little known. Yet they are and have always been the great hope of humanity.

Of course, very few of us are willing to risk our own lives to do good in this world, though we are eternally grateful to those who do. But let's try, all of us, to do our best to be number 4's. Let's help to put out the fire.

Unfortunately, one of the biggest problems at this particular point in time is that there are too few people who are working hard to douse the flames. Most people are 1's, 2's or 3's.

The 1's are the people who don't even see that the house is on fire. They don't really understand that there is a problem. They live in ignorance of the situation, consumed with the trials of everyday living. We must wake them up, educate them and ask them politely to help us put out the fire. After all, most of them are decent people. They are your friends and neighbors.

The 2's are perhaps the most frustrating. There are an awful lot of them out there. Most we would consider good people, but good people don't always do the right thing. They know that the world is on fire, but they refuse to help in any way to put it out. They just don't want to make the effort. Are they lazy? Some perhaps. Apathetic? Yes, some are just too comfortable and want to live their lives in a self-centered kind of way without bothering about the larger community. Some are just too jaded and cynical, believing that there is nothing they can do that will make any difference. Their negative outlooks defeat them before they even make an attempt to rise to the challenge. These are never the people we look up to. They are not the people who inspire, the people who win our respect. Throughout history, they have won plenty of shame, but no acclaim. These are the people to whom we must say, ultimately, "If you can't lend a hand, please get out of the way."

The 3's are good people, too. They understand the world is in trouble. They have some knowledge of what is happening. Some know too much, perhaps, and are paralyzed with fear, not knowing what to do. Some just don't have the psychological or emotional fortitude to cope with the enormity of the issues, so they avoid thinking about them or dealing with them in any way. We must help them to overcome their fears and persuade them to join us, as much as they are able, to help save the world.

The 4's and 5's, of course, are the people who conscientiously give of themselves to help others. We need more people like this. This book, hopefully, will convince you to become one (if you're not one already).

The 6's and 7's, on the other hand, are the people who are really causing problems for those of us who are working to put out the fire.

The 6's are the opportunists who take advantage of the injustices of the world to serve their own selfish interests. Usually, they are profiting in some way from the misfortunes of others. Often, these are not the nicest people you will ever meet. Many convince themselves that kindness, compassion, generosity and other human virtues are just silly notions for those who are naive. Thereby, they rationalize their destructive, harmful behavior as being "the way the world works." Their big, big egos tell them they are superior to everyone else. As such, they are living a lie, not the truth.

The 7's are the people who are deliberately setting the fire. They may even be throwing gas on it. They are knowingly involved in activities that are harmful to other people, other creatures and the planet itself. The 6's are often their minions. The 7's are not nice people either. Some would call them sociopaths. Some would call them evil. I prefer to think of them as spiritually ill. They are not well. They are suffering. They are living in ignorance of the fundamental truth of the One Idea. If we are going to heal them, and in turn ourselves, we must offer them our kindness, love, compassion, understanding and forgiveness, for our own sakes as well as theirs. Why? Because we must be true to the One Idea, the path that will lead us to a healthy place.

You've heard the saying, "the world is at sixes and sevens," meaning the world is in a state of confusion and disarray. Indeed it is. The 6's and 7's like it that way, because they are profiting from it. The rest of us, however, are in danger of being consumed by the fire. Ironically, in the end, the 6's and 7's will also be consumed. No one wins in this scenario. Everyone loses.

CHAPTER TWO

Sounding the Alarm

CHAPTER TWO

Sounding the Alarm

"We face a number of threats to our survival, from nuclear war, catastrophic global warming, genetically engineered viruses, and the number is likely to increase in the future, with the development of new technologies, and new ways things can go wrong...There is a possibility that the human race could go extinct, but it is not inevitable. This is not a prophesy of doom, but a wake-up call." ~ Stephen Hawking[5]

The world is in peril, folks. The house is on fire. We are in the midst of social, political, spiritual, economic, and environmental upheaval. This should be readily apparent to anyone who is paying attention. Scientists and other concerned, knowledgeable citizens all over the world have been sounding the alarm for decades.

"The climate alarm's been ringing for a long time. Since 1979, scores of scientists, environmentalists and diplomats have tried their best to wake people up to the issue. NASA climate scientist James Hansen outlined the 'greenhouse effect' causing the planet's warming in 1988. The following year, David Suzuki referred to global warming as 'a matter of survival.' Maurice Strong, who organized the 1992 Earth Summit in Rio warned: 'Frankly, we may get to the point where the only way of saving the world will be for industrial civilization to collapse.'"
~ Raffi Cavoukian[6]

There are a ton of articles, books, newspapers, magazines and documentary films out there that have been trying to inform us about what is happening. You'll find some of them listed in Appendix A.

"There is no longer any doubt in the expert scientific community that the Earth is warming—and it's now clear that human activity has a significant part in it." ~ Union of Concerned Scientists[7]

If you are one of those who still doesn't believe this is serious business, guess what? You're one of the number 1's! One of the deniers who still doesn't see that the house is on fire! Merrily walking past the burning house without a clue. Don't take it too hard. It's not all your fault. You may have been duped like so many others, duped by the 6's and 7's who don't have our best interests at heart, and who are taking advantage of our ignorance while increasing their wealth.

"[There is a] well-funded campaign of junk science designed to mislead the public into believing there is a split in scientific opinion about climate change. For years, this misinformation campaign has been largely funded by the oil and coal industries, working under the guise of fake grassroots groups ('astroturf groups') and industry front groups with names designed to suggest that they represent the public interest." ~ World Business Academy[8]

The purpose of this book is not to try to convince you that our planet is in big trouble. You should know that already. There are many, many others who are documenting the evidence with far more scientific expertise and firsthand knowledge than I can bring to the table here. Have you been paying attention?

Sir Martin Rees, England's Astronomer Royal, says the odds are no better than fifty-fifty that our civilization will survive to the year 2100.[9] National Geographic reports that only 10 percent of all large fish – including tuna, swordfish, halibut and flounder – are left in the sea.[10] The World Wildlife Fund laments that only 3,200 tigers remain in the wilds of Asia, compared to 100,000 just 100 years ago.[11]

When 97% of climate scientists agree that global warming is real and largely caused by human activity, shouldn't we all be paying serious attention and doing everything we can to ameliorate the situation?[12] It could take thousands and thousands of years for the planet to recover from the damage that's already been done.

"To deny that fossil fuels emit vast amounts of carbon dioxide, that carbon dioxide is accumulating in the atmosphere, that the excess carbon dioxide acts just like a greenhouse glass, and that temperatures are rising as a result is simply the equivalent of asserting the Earth is flat. Climate deniers should be viewed in the same light. The dispute over climate science is over. It's no longer news." ~ Peter Lehner, Executive Director, Natural Resources Defense Council[13]

I write this in the year 2012, a year that many belief systems regard as transitional or transformational, even cataclysmic. Interestingly, science, tradition and myth seem to be converging. Are we really facing some kind of doomsday scenario in the years ahead? No one can say for sure, but even if we are not cognizant of all of the relevant data and scientific evidence, common sense tells us that we cannot continue to overpopulate the Earth, deplete the world's resources, extract all the oil, destroy the forests, pollute the air and the water, poison our soil and our food supply without finally making the planet, at some not so distant point in the future, virtually uninhabitable for human beings and other species.

We are faced with the very real possibility that human civilization, as we now know it, is in danger of collapsing altogether. Is it a foregone conclusion? Of course not. We have to believe we can prevent the worst. And we will IF we are wise and take the necessary steps to avert disaster.

But I'm not one of those who is going to sugarcoat the truth. The path we are on right now is the path of self-destruction.

This book, then, is a call for wisdom. It is a call for immediate personal action on the part of each one of us. Time is of the essence. We must begin to look out for one another. We must think about the welfare of our children and the generations to follow. We have to grab a bucket, get in line with all of our neighbors, no matter what their race, their religion, or their political ideology, and put out the fire!

Less Than Infinity
October 31, 2011

Seven billion.
Another billion added
In only a dozen years.
Can you count a billion?
Nine zeros times 7
Means what?
Hands, fingers, stomachs, mouths
Seven (7,000,000,000) billion
Elbows
Bracing one against the other
For whatever unreasonable
Reasons
The Earth becomes cement
The sky ripped apart
The tiger, the polar bear, the elephant

Die

Bones in a graveyard
Overgrown with weeds
Distended open-mouthed babies cry
Needlessly
Choking on air
Too thick to breathe.

THE SIXTH GREAT EXTINCTION

We are in the midst of what has been called The Sixth Great Extinction.[14] Every single day, scientists estimate 150-200 species of life become extinct. This is almost 1,000 times greater than the normal rate of extinction.[15] Like the dinosaurs before us, humankind may well be among the thousands of species that now goes extinct.[16] But unlike the dinosaurs, incredibly, we will have brought about our own demise.

Imagine – all the noblest advances of human civilization and culture throughout history – gone forever! All that knowledge, science, music, art and literature – gone! All those generations that came before us, what would they think of us now? Our mothers and our fathers – who did their part to make this world a better place – for our sakes – bit by bit, century upon century? For what?

It is up to us now. What kind of people are we? Are we so selfish, greedy and cruel that we would throw it all away? We are the last generation with a real opportunity to save the world.

We must wake up. Our complacent dream is over. Our nightmare has begun. In the horrific future that we are now creating, human beings may have to revert to some kind of desperate feudal or Stone Age existence – if they survive at all.

All those wild and crazy science fiction stories of decades past may turn out to be fairly accurate foretellings of a very real future. *Mad Max* was a horrific vision of a dog-eat-dog world with limited technology and resources. *Dune* showed us a desert planet where water was more precious than gold. George Orwell's *1984* imagined an oppressive propagandistic surveillance state with "Thought Police" that sought to control even an individual's ability to think. *Brave New World* was a vision of a hedonistic society where human beings were created in a lab and assigned by the World State to specific social castes to perform specific functions. Words like love, marriage, and family were vulgarities no one dared utter in polite company, and whenever life became the least bit challenging, all one had to do was pop a pill to mask the pain. And then there was that *Twilight Zone* episode called "The Midnight Sun" where the world was overheating, getting unbearably hotter and hotter and hotter – and in the freakish scenario that unfolded – colder and colder and colder. These fanciful visions now don't seem so far-fetched at all.

LOOKING INTO THE FUTURE

Scientists can only tell us so much. The facts can always be spun, debated and interpreted in every which way, but it doesn't take much imagination to see into the future that potentially lies before us. We know that climate change will bring droughts, floods, fires, earthquakes, tornadoes, and inundations of coastlines and low-lying islands.[17]

If we don't decisively address our energy needs in a sustainable way, we will find ourselves in an increasingly nightmarish landscape on the planet. Right now our entire way of life is based on petroleum. As fossil fuel resources diminish and become prohibitively expensive, economies are in danger of collapsing altogether. Without jobs, more and more people will become homeless. Access to food and clean, fresh water will become more and more difficult. There will be widespread famine and disease. Tensions and conflicts will skyrocket in an already conflicted world divided by religion and race and access to resources. Crime will increase.

There will be wars, wars involving not only conventional weapons, but also nuclear,[18] chemical and biological weapons. Cyber terrorists may well have the capability to shut down power grids and bring everyday commerce to an abrupt halt. No, it doesn't take much imagination to envision a world gone completely mad. Is that where we're heading? When the smoke finally clears, who or what will be left alive?

Of course, none of us can know at this point what exactly will happen, but everyone ought to be able to agree that we need to be smart, make wise choices, and do everything we can to diminish the pain and suffering that lurk down the road.

"In every deliberation, we must consider the impact on the seventh generation." ~ The Great Law of the Iroquois

Hopefully, mankind will survive the consequences of his own folly. It won't be easy. One of the reasons I felt compelled to write this book is for those future generations who do survive, so that they might find their way, pick up the pieces and create a world that finally works. That world must be founded on love. That world must acknowledge, respect, and live the One Idea.

The One Idea can save us, and it may be the only thing that can.

CHAPTER THREE

The One Idea

CHAPTER THREE

The One Idea

Ok, so what is it? The One Idea that saves the world?

You already know what it is. We all know what it is. It's a very, very old idea. And it's so simple. No doubt it goes all the way back to our earliest ancestors when humankind first began to understand our place in the world. It's an idea that is a part of every major religion, and it is acknowledged by atheists and agnostics as well. Because within this idea you can find the moral center of the Universe, the ethical guideline for living, whether you believe in a God or not. You might say it is the place where science and religion intersect and truly find compatibility.

Are you ready? Here it is.

The One Idea:

We are One.

That's it. That's the One Idea.

But you knew that already. Of course you did. We all know this great truth in our hearts.

This idea has been expressed over and over again by artists, poets, musicians, scientists and philosophers and every great spiritual teacher. It is, I believe, the one idea that can bring all of us together, or at least most of us – if we really commit to it and heed its implications.

Even though we've heard it many times before, we have chosen to ignore its great fundamental truth. We have refused to really grasp what it means and what it requires of all of us. We conveniently set it aside in our daily lives as we go about satisfying our own individual ego needs, petty and disrespectful as they so often are.

The times are such that we can no longer behave like children who think only of themselves. We have to finally grow up as a species. We have to become responsible adults.

We ignore the One Idea at our own peril. Without it, we are lost. But if we really live it, we will indeed save the world, no matter how trying our physical circumstances become. It may well be our last chance and last hope.

The house is on fire. The One Idea shows us the way to put the fire out.

Wait a minute! What does it really mean, this oneness, and what does it imply? "Ay," as Hamlet would say, "there's the rub."[19]

First of all, we must understand that we are part of a whole – everything is interconnected.

"We are all connected, to each other biologically, to the Earth chemically, to the rest of the universe atomically."
~ Neil deGrasse Tyson[20]

There is unity in all things. So everything we do has ramifications throughout the entire system. All of our actions have subtle effects, like ripples in a pond. These effects are mostly unseen by you or me, yet they ripple throughout the entire Universe.

Okay, that's huge, isn't it? Let that sink in a bit.

"You're not just a drop in the ocean, you're also the mighty ocean in the drop." ~ Rumi

PART OF THE WHOLE

Each of us is a part of this whole. You might think of the Universe as a human body. I might be one tiny atom in the thumbnail of that universal body and you might be an atom in the left kneecap. (Or wherever you like. Pick your own body part. Be creative!) But though there is a seemingly huge distance between me in the thumbnail and you in the left kneecap, we are still part of the same body.

Part of the problem we face today is that we tend to believe in the illusion instead of the truth. The illusion is that everything we see is separate, but the truth is that it is all an interconnected part of a whole.

Take food, for example, we think we can pull a vitamin out and put it in a pill and it will do the same thing as when we ingest it in its natural state with food. Scientists are finding, however, that everything interacts. When you start to split the whole into separate parts, there are consequences. The parts do not function the same when separated out as when they are part of the whole.

Likewise, if one animal goes extinct, there will be ramifications throughout the ecosystem and a domino effect of species depletion may occur.

Perhaps naturalist John Muir expressed it best, "When we try to pick out anything by itself, we find it hitched to everything else in the universe."[21]

I'm going to say something very important here and I don't want you to miss it:

If we are going to preserve the viability of life on this planet, we must strive to understand the connections, the interrelatedness of all things.

"The saddest aspect of life right now is that science gathers knowledge faster than society gathers wisdom." ~ Isaac Asimov

Our science and technology are advancing rapidly, but our ability to understand the interconnected ramifications of the application of the technology is not keeping pace. Wisdom is required. We must become aware of the consequences for any alterations we humans might make to the natural world.

ONE HUMAN FAMILY

"Many problems that confront us today are created by man, whether they are violent conflicts, destruction of the environment, poverty or hunger. These problems can be resolved thanks to human efforts by understanding that we are brother and sister and by developing this sense of closeness. We must cultivate a

universal responsibility toward each other and extend it to the planet that we have to share." ~ His Holiness, The Dalai Lama

The One Idea compels us to consider our relationship as human beings. We are all, in fact, one family. Science and most religions agree that we are all descended from common ancestors. That makes us all cousins. We all share the same many times great grandparents at some point back in history.

As a genealogist, I have studied thousands of families and their ancestral lines going far back in time. It is very clear to me that we do indeed share common ancestors and not as far back as you would think. Unfortunately, most people are not able to trace very far back. The connections from generation to generation have been lost; the records were not kept. But those of us who can trace a long way back in time often find that we do connect at some point and share common ancestry.

This is not at all surprising when you consider the mathematics. With every generation, the number of your grandparents doubles. Starting with yourself as the first generation, you have four grandparents. Then at your next generation back (generation 2), you have 8 great grandparents—four on your father's side and four on your mother's side. At generation 3 you have 16 great great grandparents, at generation 4 you have 32 3rd great grandparents, and so on.

By the time you get to the 35th generation, you have about 32 billion grandparents. How far back is 35 generations? That will vary depending on your age. For me, my 35th generation goes all the way back to Charlemagne, the Father of Kings (c. 742-814 CE).

This is nothing unusual. Most people of European ancestry are likely descended from Charlemagne. He had several wives and concubines and many children. His progeny became the kings and queens and nobles of Europe.

When I first discovered this part of my ancestry many years ago, I was amazed. You mean little me was actually descended from Charlemagne?! The more I investigated, the more I discovered I was related in some way to a whole bunch of famous people throughout history and it began to dawn on me that there was nothing unique about it at all. We are all connected to these people. We are all descended from the kings and queens or the great tribal leaders of our various cultures.

But let's go back to the math for a minute. At the 35th generation you have about 32 billion grandparents, but there were only about 300 million people on the entire planet at that time, the time of Charlemagne.[22] How can that be? How can you have more grandparents than there were people on the planet?

The reason is that not all of those grandparents are different individuals. If you look at Charlemagne, for example, you will find that you don't descend from just one of his children, you descend from a number of his many children. These children obviously share the same grandparents.

Now let's take the 50th generation occurring about the first century CE. At that level, you have about 2 quadrillion grandparents, yet there were only about 200 million people on the planet. The numbers alone suggest that the majority of us must share a common ancestry at some point not that far back in time.

My own research shows that many of us of European-American descent share common ancestry at about the year 1300 CE, the time of King Edward I of England. So our common ancestors often include not only Charlemagne, but Alfred the Great, King Malcolm III of Scotland, and many of the kings and queens of ancient England, Scotland, Ireland, France, and Spain.

Before we get too full of ourselves, however, boasting about our relationship to the royals, let's be honest. Many of those kings and queens were pretty ruthless people and, in many ways, not the most worthy of our admiration. A humble heart in service of humanity is always more impressive and laudable than some overbearing overlord.

You might be asking why is everyone descended from royalty and not from ordinary people? Oh, but we are descended from so-called "ordinary" people. The vast majority of our ancestors were not famous in any way, but most of those connections are lost, because few records have survived. The royalty and the well-to-do are the only people for whom we can find fairly accurate records of their lineages, mostly documented in inheritances, transfers of land, and other histories. The "commoners" didn't even have surnames until about 1300-1500 CE, so there is little hope of tracing any of those lines back any further, except through DNA.

Recent studies of DNA, by the way, are fascinating. The science shows we all share common ancestors in Africa, our genetic Adam and Eve.

"... we share a common ancestry with every living thing on Earth. DNA ties us all together, so we share ancestry with barracuda and bacteria and mushrooms, if you go far enough back, over a billion years." ~ Spencer Wells, Population Geneticist[23]

There's the One Idea again. Interconnectedness. We are genetically linked not only to humanity, but also to every living thing on Earth. We are One.

THE ILLUSION OF SEPARATENESS

Unfortunately, our consciousness has a long way to go before we truly evolve to our highest potential as human beings, yet the urgency of our times requires that we awaken quickly.

"A human being is part of a whole, called by us 'Universe,' a part limited in time and space. He experiences himself, his thoughts and feelings as something separated from the rest – a kind of optical delusion of his consciousness. This delusion is a kind of prison for us... Our task must be to free ourselves from this prison by widening our circle of compassion to embrace all living creatures and the whole of nature in its beauty." ~ Albert Einstein[24]

The great paradox is that while we are all connected in this universal body or whole, we are, at the same time, all independent individuals. At least we appear to be. But we're not really independent; we are interdependent. The separateness is an illusion. Too many conveniently "forget" that they are part of the whole, believing that their actions have little or no bearing on the lives of others.

Fiber

We forget that air
is a substance
we can't see it
but it's there
connecting everything

and everyone

With every breath
i take you in
give back myself
we are in touch
no matter how far

The distance an illusion
between that which is
not and can not be
separated.

Many of our problems arise from the illusion of separateness, that we are disconnected from one another. It's easy to do harm to someone you don't know or who you believe is not important to you or your life, someone you feel is inferior to you. War, hatred, and violence all spring from one infernal idea: that one person, race, creed, or culture is better than another.

The truth of the One Idea, however, must be recognized. We Are One. We are all interconnected and interdependent on one another for our well-being. This bears repeating over and over and over again, until it becomes a part of our everyday consciousness. Yes, every single day. From moment to moment we must be aware of our relationships to our brothers and sisters. Especially when we are in potential situations of conflict, we must remind ourselves of our interconnection and act with compassion.

THE IMPORTANCE OF THE INDIVIDUAL

Even though we are One, that doesn't diminish the importance of the individual. In fact, the One Idea emphasizes the importance of individualism.

We are all different. We all have different gifts and different ways of contributing to the whole. No one is superior to another. You wouldn't say my right leg is more important than my left, would you? Or my ear is better than my eye? No. All the parts of the body contribute to the functioning of the whole.

The same is true of our world. There is no such thing as an insignificant life, only the insignificance of mind that refuses to grasp the implications.

Each of us has a very important role to play in a healthy, sustainable world. It is in all of our best interests to foster the development and growth of each individual. All of us should be encouraged to be the best we can be, to contribute all the good that each of us has to offer. None of us should be engaged in activities that deliberately diminish or harm others.

> *"All mankind is tied together; all life is interrelated, and we are all caught in an inescapable network of mutuality, tied in a single garment of destiny. Whatever affects one directly, affects all indirectly... I can never be what I ought to be until you are what you ought to be. And you can never be what you ought to be until I am what I ought to be – this is the interrelated structure of reality."* ~ Rev. Dr. Martin Luther King, Jr.[25]

Now, if any one culture, or religion, or other specific group of people considers itself better than everyone else and engages in activities that will harm others, then we have a problem, don't we? Self-righteousness is a big problem – people who think they are right and everyone else is wrong. We're really talking about ego, self-centeredness, and intolerance.

> *"Being tolerant does not mean that I share another one's belief. But it does mean that I acknowledge another one's right to believe, and obey, his own conscience."* ~ Viktor Frankl

Extremism is marked by a closed mind and a meanness of spirit – unwilling to listen, unwilling to reason, unwilling to compromise, unwilling to forgive, and in the end, unwilling to learn and unwilling to grow.

The purveyors of hatred and intolerance must attack the very idea of tolerance itself lest they see themselves for what they truly are. On the other hand, those of us who oppose hateful bigotry must not be silent when it rears its ugly head. When the tolerant tolerate the intolerant they risk losing the very freedoms they are trying to protect. Bigotry should never be allowed to become acceptable and commonplace in a healthy society.

The One Idea reminds us that no one is inferior or superior to another. And the same goes for the plants and the animals. Every being has its own important and unique place in the cosmic dance.

LOVE

"Love is patient; love is kind; love is not envious or boastful or arrogant or rude. It does not insist on its own way; it is not irritable or resentful; it does not rejoice in wrongdoing, but rejoices in the truth. It bears all things, believes all things, hopes all things, endures all things." ~ 1 Corinthians 13:4-7

Love is the great truth we all know in our hearts and must eventually recognize. Love is inherent in the One Idea. Since we are all one, part of a collective whole, to love another is to love yourself.

"Thou shalt love thy neighbor as thyself." ~ Leviticus 19:18

Conversely, to hate another is to hate yourself. Hatred is self-destructive and will only bring pain and sorrow to the whole. We all know this; we've known it forever, yet we continue our selfish, immature ways and take a perverse delight in inflicting pain on others.

Sadly, our world is now so divided, so distrustful, so fearful that we are bringing about our own childish destruction.

"Love is the only sane and satisfactory answer to the problem of human existence." ~ Erich Fromm[26]

The need for love is central to the teachings of all the world's great religions. Love redeems and heals the world. The only question is, by the time we finally take this simple truth to heart and really begin to live it (if we ever do), will it be too late?

How important is love? We all know that the best things in life are all about love, don't we? The things we say we love are the things that make our lives worth living: good music, good food, good friends. Positive, loving relationships make for the happiest of lives. Negative, disturbing relationships make for pain and suffering.

> *"The first peace, which is the most important, is that which comes within the souls of people when they realize their relationship, their oneness, with the universe and all its Powers, and when they realize that at the center of the universe dwells Wakan-Tanka [the Great Spirit], and that this center is really everywhere, it is within each of us."* ~ Black Elk, Oglala Lakota[27]

Love is the message of all of the great spiritual teachers, all of the enlightened ones, throughout history. It is so simple to understand intellectually, but so difficult to live emotionally and spiritually. There is probably no greater challenge in this life than to love others unconditionally. To get to a better place both on an individual and a collective societal level, we need to really commit to it. We must live it.

> *"For the first time in my life I saw the truth as it is set into song by so many poets, proclaimed as the final wisdom by so many thinkers. The truth – that Love is the ultimate and highest goal to which man can aspire. Then I grasped the meaning of the greatest secret that human poetry and human thought and belief have to impart: The salvation of man is through love and in love."*
> ~ Viktor Frankl[28]

COMPASSION AND EMPATHY

> *"The whole idea of compassion is based on a keen awareness of the interdependence of all these living beings, which are all part of one another, and all involved in one another."* ~ Thomas Merton, Trappist monk and author[29]

Love is a big word, of course, used in many different ways, and often trivialized. Many people are more comfortable with the word compassion. Webster's defines compassion as "a feeling of deep sympathy and sorrow for another who is stricken by misfortune, accompanied by a strong desire to alleviate the suffering."[30]

Compassion requires the ability to empathize, to identify with another person's situation and to be able to experience his or her pain and suffering on some level. It's about understanding; it's about knowing what it's like to be in someone else's shoes.

As an actor, I have spent much of my life literally walking in other people's shoes. That's what creating a character is all about. You need to get inside a character's skin, feel what he feels, and think what he thinks. Likewise, as a writer and a poet, I need to be able to think and feel what others do in order to be able to create my art and speak truth.

Empathy and compassion are very desirable qualities in a human being. Those who lack these qualities are what I would call "heartless." Others would say they are sociopathic or psychopathic, the sorts of people who are prevalent among the 6's and 7's and who are willfully contributing to the destruction of our world.

No matter what word we use – love, compassion, empathy – it's really all about caring, isn't it? Caring not only for ourselves, but for all living things.

Because we care, because we love, we must act. Ignoring the problems and hoping or pretending that they will go away is foolhardy.

Love is active, not passive. It is our love for one another, for Mother Earth, for our fellow creatures that compels us to act on their behalf.

Love is protective. A mother doesn't stand idly by when she senses her child is in danger. She springs into action, ready to defend the life of the child with her own.

Each of us must do no less. Each of us must spring to the defense, and take necessary action for the sake of all. Doing nothing as our house burns to the ground is not acceptable. Doing nothing only enables the status quo and as every informed citizen knows, the status quo of this modern-day world is destroying what we hold most dear.

"It is time to combat the ignorance that inspires hatred and fear...
now let us bear witness to the power of compassion."
~ Karen Armstrong, author, founder of the Charter for Compassion[31]

And make no mistake. To be compassionate requires great strength of character. It is never weakness. The people who stand for compassion and love often do so at the risk of their own lives. They are among the 5's, the people we admire most who remain true to themselves at all costs and true to the highest principles of human decency in the face of unspeakable cruelty.

THE GOLDEN RULE

Do unto others...

The Golden Rule is also inherent in the One Idea. Because we are One, parts of a whole, because we are all connected, we must, for our own sakes and out of consideration for others, cultivate empathy and compassion. We must live by The Golden Rule, treating others as we would like to be treated ourselves.

The Golden Rule[32] has been expressed in many different ways in many different religions and philosophies:

"Do unto others as you would have them do unto you."
~ Matthew 7:12 (Christianity)

"Hurt not others in ways that you yourself would find hurtful."
~ Udanavarga 5:18 (Buddhism)

"Do not do to others what would cause pain if done to you."
~ Mahabharata 5:1517 (Hinduism)

"Thou shalt not avenge, nor bear any grudge against the children of thy people, but thou shalt love thy neighbour as thyself..."
~ Leviticus 19:18 (Judaism, Christianity)

"None of you truly believes until he wishes for his brother what he wishes for himself." ~ An-Nawawi's Forty Hadith 13, p. 56 (Islam)

"Just as pain is not agreeable to you, it is so with others. Knowing this principle of equality treat others with respect and compassion." ~ Suman Suttam , verse 150 (Jainism)

"And if thine eyes be turned towards justice, choose thou for thy neighbour that which thou choosest for thyself." ~ Bahá'u'lláh (Bahá'í Faith)

"The basis of Sufism is consideration of the hearts and feelings of others. If you haven't the will to gladden someone's heart, then at least beware lest you hurt someone's heart, for on our path, no sin exists but this." ~ Dr. Javad Nurbakhsh, Master of the Nimatullahi Sufi Order (Sufism)

"Regard your neighbor's gain as your own gain, and your neighbor's loss as your own loss." ~ T'ai Shang Kan Ying P'ien (Taoism)

"Do not kill or injure your neighbor, for it is not him that you injure, you injure yourself. But do good to him, therefore add to his days of happiness as you add to your own. Do not wrong or hate your neighbor, for it is not him that you wrong, you wrong yourself." ~ Golden Rule of the Shawnee

"Don't do things you wouldn't want to have done to you." ~ British Humanist Society

"Be charitable to all beings, love is the representative of God." ~ Ko-ji-ki Hachiman Kasuga (Shinto)

"Whatever is disagreeable to yourself do not do unto others." ~ Shayast-na-Shayast 13:29 (Zoroastrianism)

"Never impose on others what you would not choose for yourself." ~ Confucius

"What thou avoidest suffering thyself seek not to impose on others." ~ Epictetus, Greek philosopher

"Do not do to others that which would anger you if others did it to you." ~ Socrates (Greece; 5th century BCE)

"Do not to your neighbor what you would take ill from him."
~ Pittacus, one of the seven sages of Greece

"And as ye would that men should do to you, do ye also to them likewise." ~ Luke 6:31 (Christianity)

"Seek for mankind that of which you are desirous for yourself, that you may be a believer; treat well as a neighbor the one who lives near you, that you may be a Muslim [one who submits to God]." ~ Sukhanan-i-Muhammad, Teheran, 1938 (Islam)

"All things are our relatives; what we do to everything, we do to ourselves. All is really One." ~ Black Elk, Oglala Lakota

"That which is hateful to you, do not do to your fellow. That is the whole Torah; the rest is the explanation; go and learn." ~ Talmud, Shabbat 31a (Judaism)

The Golden Rule, however it is expressed, provides a simple guideline for healthy human interaction and behavior. It represents a universal truth and a moral imperative. It may have become trivialized in our society and mocked by the heartless, the jaded and the cynical, but most of us recognize in our heart of hearts that when we hurt another, we also hurt ourselves. Those who would deny this truth are truly lost souls. Their spiritual illness, their psychological and emotional distress, is profound and pitiable.

The Golden Rule. It's so simple, but how many of us actually live it? That's the problem, isn't it? Too many people and too many institutions don't treat us the way we would like to be treated. It's too easy to be rude and disrespectful. We see it all the time in American culture. It's become "cool" to be mean and abusive.

Can we actually turn this around? I think so. I certainly hope so. But it will require a determined act of will on the part of each of us. Compassion is not something that comes to us automatically. At our worst, we can be very selfish and cruel creatures. Compassion has to be taught, nurtured and cultivated. It is really about personal commitment.

I made a formal commitment myself by affirming The Charter for Compassion which was created in 2009 as a result of author

Karen Armstrong's 2008 TED Prize wish. See Appendix B for more on the Charter.

By committing ourselves to compassion, it becomes a part of our daily consciousness. We become very aware of how we treat others. We may not be perfect all the time, but we recognize when we are being less compassionate than we could be.

In short, The Golden Rule shows the way to a healthy and happy society.

STAR STUFF

The cosmologist Carl Sagan said, "We are made of star stuff." I like that. We are part of the vast mystery of this Universe. The stars themselves are within us. We are made of the same ancient, timeless stuff.

> *"Every atom in your body came from a star that exploded. And the atoms in your left hand probably came from a different star than your right hand. It really is the most poetic thing I know about physics. You are all stardust."* ~ Lawrence Krauss, theoretical physicist[33]

There's something awesome, cosmic, and illimitable about who we are. Have we come close to realizing our potential? Anything is possible. We can save the world. It is certainly within our power. All it takes is imagination and the will to proceed.

Interconnection. Love. Compassion. The Golden Rule. These are all part of the One Idea. We are One. All is One. This is the truth. We've known it all along, but now we can't afford to dismiss it. We must live it.

CHAPTER FOUR

The World
at
Sixes and Sevens

CHAPTER FOUR

The World at Sixes and Sevens

Now we are really beginning to understand the One Idea and all it implies about the ethical treatment of others. Our own personal well-being is dependent on the well-being of others. If my neighbor is in pain and suffering, I will ultimately suffer, too. This global interconnectedness compels us to care about one another, to have empathy and compassion.

"Our sorrows and wounds are healed only when we touch them with compassion." ~ The Buddha

If I want to heal myself, I need to be part of an effort that heals you as well. We can all think of times when the loving comfort of others was profoundly healing to us. If we really want to get along, we should practice the Golden Rule in all areas of our lives. This is really common sense, isn't it?

So what is preventing us from doing the right thing?

That's a fairly complex question. Everything is interconnected, remember? There are many contributing factors. Each of us needs to be aware of the extent to which we are personally contributing to the collective illness of the planet. Then, we must take steps to rectify, to heal and balance, our own relationship to the Universe of which we are a part.

AN AMERICAN PERSPECTIVE

In this chapter, we're going to take a look at some of the truly dark forces that are leading us down the path of global self-destruction.

Anyone who is paying any attention recognizes that the whole world is at sixes and sevens, in a state of extreme confusion, and on the verge, perhaps, of unimaginable chaos and suffering. Let's not diminish the importance of this hour.

My perspective throughout this book is, of course, as a United States citizen.[34] I suspect similar phenomena that I shall describe here are happening all over. You from other lands may have different experiences, but as you read this book, ask yourself if what I'm seeing is true in your part of the world as well.

In the U.S., people no longer know whom to trust. They have lost faith in their political leaders, their institutions, and their media. Through fear mongering and shameless propaganda, these powerful entities, in pursuing their political, social, and economic agendas, have successfully divided the American people, separating us into different factions, inspiring hatred and distrust of one another.

"Abuse of words has been the great instrument of sophistry and chicanery, of party, faction, and division of society."
~ John Adams[35]

Through the use of deliberate, highly effective marketing tactics, labels and slogans, various groups of people are being demonized in our culture, including immigrants, the poor, the unemployed, African Americans, Muslims, Christians, Jews, women, gays, intellectuals, teachers, union members, peacemakers, environmentalists, etc.

"Once you label me, you negate me."
~ Søren Kierkegaard, philosopher

The demonization is so intense that people think of those with different views as being evil. Hatred of "the other" has become brazenly visible and commonplace in our politics and in our culture.

There is very little reasonable or compassionate communication taking place to span the political, social, and ethnic divides. This is largely the result of so much misinformation and disinformation being disseminated by the powerful, the unscrupulous and the ignorant. People in opposing camps can't even agree on the facts, because each side has its own set of "facts." And too many of these "facts" are just plain lies.

"We can have facts without thinking but we cannot have thinking without facts." ~ John Dewey, educator and philosopher

Good Guys and Bad Guys

Who wears the black hat and who the white?
Is evil so easy to recognize?
Can you see inside the shadow of a man's eyes
Who he really is?
Is one man's enemy another man's hero?
We fight with such conviction
These comic book villains who don't really

Exist

Perhaps, by looking in, instead of out
We'd find the very thing we hate
And making peace with that incorrigible

Demon

Set ourselves free
The longed-for hope of humanity
Realized in an instant of unqualified

Reflection.

Lacking any political unity, the people are finding it almost impossible to come together and make any effective common sense change. Of course, that's exactly what the 6's and 7's want. They don't want people making waves. They want people to submit, to be so splintered, fearful and demoralized that they are incapable of mounting any sort of resistance to the status quo.

"Nothing strengthens authority so much as silence."
~ Leonardo da Vinci

People are afraid – and for good reason. There is much to fear in a world that is on fire, rapidly approaching environmental and economic turmoil.

"Those who can make you believe absurdities can make you commit atrocities." ~ Voltaire[36]

When people are afraid they are indeed capable of committing atrocities. As they become more and more financially destitute, they will strike out in order to survive. Let's prevent the situation from becoming so desperate.

Fear is best combated with love, understanding, education and reason. Before we can properly attack the fire, we've got to make an honest assessment of the situation. Let's take a deep breath and try to understand what is happening. Why is our world in such a predicament? Why are we so divided? Why can't we all come together and do what is necessary to put out the fire?

Religion and politics are two of the main areas of human experience that keep us passionately divided. We all know the old saying, "Don't discuss religion or politics, especially when you're visiting your relatives!" This is a sage piece of advice, because religion and politics are so personal. They go right to the core of who we are and what we believe. Relationships can be severely damaged or even destroyed by religious and political arguments. If you begin to challenge or attack someone's personal belief systems, you will be met with stubborn and perhaps abusive antagonism.

When we look at what's wrong with the world, we've got to begin by looking at religion, politics and the institutions that we have created, the systems and structures that manipulate our perceptions, hold us prisoner and keep us from being free.

RELIGION

Much of the conflict in our world today is religiously based. Throughout history, religions have been the cause of much misery, cruelty and suffering. Today, as always, we find religious extremists committing atrocities against their fellows in the name of religion.

Religion has also been, and can be, a great force for good.

Individuals and small groups of people are usually responsible for the heinous acts of violence. We should not blame entire religions for the egregious behaviors of a few. But let me say this unequivocally: any church or religious group that preaches hatred of other people, no matter who they are, and advocates violence against certain groups of people, for whatever reason, is profoundly spiritually ill itself.

We are One. To hurt another is to hurt yourself.

Healthy religion is never about hatred. It is always about kindness, love and spiritual growth. It is about doing what is good for the entire community.

"Nobody should seek his own good, but the good of others."
~ 1 Corinthians 10:24

Healthy religion is also open-minded and respectful of others' religious beliefs. All religious institutions should be promoting love and peace in their congregations – at all times.

I will talk more about religion and how we can make peace with our different belief systems in the next chapter.

POLITICS, POLITICIANS AND POLITICAL PARTIES

"Politics, it seems to me, for years, or all too long, has been concerned with right or left instead of right or wrong."
~ Richard Armour, poet and author

Most Americans these days are so sick of politics, they make a concerted effort to avoid anything political. They are sick of all the politicians and their political parties, and sick as well of all the political operatives, pundits and game players. They recognize that all these political types are not the most distinguished, reputable or trustworthy

THE WORLD AT SIXES AND SEVENS

people in the world. There are an awful lot of 6's and 7's in the political arena.

Think about it. What sort of person wants to be a politician? Certainly, most of us aren't cut out for it. Politicians have to be sycophantic, evasive, informative, inspiring, seemingly truthful, charismatic, and duplicitous all at the same time. We should never look to our politicians to tell us what is ethical and right. They will say whatever they need to say to pander to any particular audience. Politicians live in a world of buzzwords and banalities, but rarely do they speak the honest truth.

In order to get elected, politicians have to find ways to distinguish themselves in the minds of voters. This usually involves trumpeting their own "virtues," while trashing their competitors. Politics is a nasty business. You won't find much love and compassion there. Ruthless people can do very well in politics, but most good guys finish last.

It's a sad situation, isn't it? Worst of all, when the citizens are so fed up and disgusted, they withdraw from any civic participation in their government. Huge numbers of people refuse even to vote. As a result, nothing ever changes and we get more of the same.

If we are going to get any real change, huge numbers of us must get passionately involved and fight for what we believe in.

"Politics ought to be the part-time profession of every citizen who would protect the rights and privileges of free people and who would preserve what is good and fruitful in our national heritage." ~ Dwight D. Eisenhower[37]

Me, I still believe in American democracy. I believe in government "of the people, by the people, and for the people." But We the People have got to get involved quick, before we lose the precious freedoms our Founding Fathers gave us.

At the close of the Constitutional Convention in 1787, as Benjamin Franklin was leaving Independence Hall, a lady asked him what kind of government we now had. "A republic," he replied, "if you can keep it." [38]

Money – Big Money – has totally corrupted American politics. It takes huge amounts of cash to run for office. Unless you're personally very well off, you stand little chance of ever achieving high political office. This is simply wrong in a democracy. We ought to be looking for leaders with integrity and character from every class, gender and ethnic background. Instead, we too often get the game-playing, power-hungry people who see everything through dollar signs and what's in it for them and their buddies.

Look at our national leaders. Who are they? For the most part, we have a bunch of millionaires and billionaires who run our government and our media. Do you think they really understand or care about the needs of ordinary Americans? And who's behind them anyway? Who funds their campaigns? Who's pulling their strings? A bunch of huge corporations, Big Banks, Wall Street gamblers, and extremely wealthy individuals who are all making heaps of money off the exploitation of us all. They like the system just fine as it is. It works for them, but it doesn't work for the vast majority of the American people.

THE MEDIA

When I use the word "media" in this book, I'm primarily referring to the mainstream corporate media – TV, radio, newspapers and magazines – from which most Americans currently obtain much of their understanding about current events.

Thriving on conflict and drama, these media love the circus atmosphere of our politics and our elections. After all, who rakes in the billions of dollars spent on political advertising? The media! They have a financial interest in stoking the fires of political antagonism. They are intentionally trying to divide us and they are succeeding. It's not a very reputable way to make money, is it? Turning people against one another. Appealing to the worst in people instead of the best.

As they concentrate their efforts on making a buck, the media do the public a grave disservice by not taking the time to confront politicians on the issues. They ought to be helping the public to distinguish between facts and propaganda. They ought to be promoting reasonable debate.

Whatever happened to being objective and telling the truth? Isn't that what the media are supposed to do when they cover the news?

TELEVISION

Television probably has more influence over people's lives than any other medium. The technology of television could have been used as a great force for good, to educate, as well as entertain, but greed and commercial interests have totally corrupted its once bright promise.

Make no mistake: television is now an advertising medium. It's primary reason for being is the buying and selling of products and services. In between commercials, you can watch any number of inane, sometimes trashy, vulgar absurdities that pass themselves off as "entertainment." What little educational, intellectual and artistic merit television used to have has now almost entirely vanished.

Every day, all over the country, Americans are bombarded with commercial messages. Buy this, buy that. You need this "such and so" to be cool, to be sexy, to be fulfilled. It's all nonsense, of course, yet this is the lie we put into our own and, more insidiously, our children's heads – daily. We are not raising healthy, well-adjusted, compassionate human beings; we are raising consumers. The implicit message is "if you're not buying all the latest nifty stuff, you're a loser." And in order to buy all this stuff, you have to have lots of money, right?

But we all know money can't buy happiness. Accumulating a whole bunch of useless stuff won't cure what ails our emotional and spiritual selves.

Happiness comes from healthy, positive relationships with others in your life and the world around you.

If you've got loving relationships, food to eat, a roof over your head, work that is meaningful, and a healthy mind and body, guess what? You're going to be a happy human being. That's the simple truth. And it doesn't take much "stuff" at all.

"A man is rich in proportion to the number of things he can afford to let alone." ~ Henry David Thoreau[39]

How would our world be different if television were used for education and learning? What if it made us aware of the truth of what is happening in the world? What if it provided ways to discuss the issues and find solutions? What if it worked to bring people together, to promote peace and understanding, rather than to divide us? Instead we have turned TV into a tawdry marketplace, an intellectual wasteland.

Sadly, in our addictive culture, television has become one more addictive drug. People are mesmerized into quiet submission, conformity and indifference. They turn on the TV to provide noise to fill the disturbing silences and emotional voids in their own lives. They plop their children in front of it for hours on end to "babysit," a poor substitute for the nurturing and care-giving that every child has every right to expect from his/her parents.

There is the old saying, "you are what you eat." The adage is true not only for what we put into our bodies, but also for what we put into our minds. Most of what TV delivers is complete garbage – junk food for the mind, heart, and soul – with no nutritional value. It's like eating cotton candy. Sure, the first few bites are tasty, but keep eating the stuff and you're going to get very, very sick.

THE NEWS MEDIA

Even our television news has become junk food. It's not really news at all. It's infotainment. We are fed a steady diet of conflict, violence and mean-spirited hate of any number of "others," with too little reason and too little sanity to balance the negative effects on our psyches.

The media are supposed to deliver the important news, the truth about the state of the world, the critical issues that affect all of our lives. They have a responsibility to alert us all to the dangers we face and to moderate a dialogue among divergent points of view to ascertain the facts and aid us in finding ethical, workable solutions.

Instead, journalistic standards of integrity, the heart and soul of the profession, have gone by the wayside. Sources are not checked, facts are distorted, pundits are not challenged. In short, much of what we get is propaganda or outright lying. Truth gets little attention, especially if that truth reflects negatively on the corporate world.

Did you know that only six major companies control most of the media in the United States?[40] This should be of great concern to every freedom-loving American, for those who control and shape the information we receive can basically control the way we think.

"Half the world is composed of people who have something to say and can't, and the other half who have nothing to say and keep on saying it." ~ Robert Frost

Our world is on fire! Human civilization is in serious trouble, but you wouldn't know it from watching the hunky-dory nonsense we see on TV. Perhaps much worse than what the media does tell us is what they don't tell us. By deliberately omitting or minimizing important stories, information and facts, they are shaping public opinion to serve their own purposes, which are often at odds with the public good.

If the media did their job, the people would be up in arms, demanding accountability, and I wouldn't have to write this book!

It's time we all recognize that the "news," whether slanted to the political right or the left, is predominantly concerned with satisfying a corporate agenda. That corporate agenda is to maximize profits. They discovered that there wasn't any big money in doing real news, with real investigative reporters, so they turned all their efforts into more profit-making ventures, creating carnival sideshows with lots of "sound and fury signifying nothing."[41]

Meanwhile, the newspapers and other print media that used to be actively involved in disseminating valuable information to the public have been failing and going out of business. They aren't making enough money to survive. It all comes down to money again, doesn't it?

The public press has been called the Fourth Estate. They play an extremely important role in a healthy democracy. In a free society, the media are not part of the government; they are free to take a good hard look at the government and hold it accountable. In fact, by exposing the transgressions of the three branches of government – executive, legislative, and judicial – and demanding accountability, the Fourth Estate is the greatest protector of the rights and liberties of ordinary citizens.

The Fourth Estate in America used to be a strong defender of the common good, but it has been so corrupted by moneyed corporate and political special interest that it no longer holds the faith and trust of the American people.

This is an untenable situation for freedom and democracy.

Fortunately, there are still some news organizations out there that employ real journalists who dedicate their lives to serving the public interest. The work they do is invaluable and often requires tremendous fortitude and courage. They need our encouragement and support.

But what about the less principled people who work for and own these money-grubbing corporate media giants? Why don't they care?

That's a good question. Why don't they care?

Hang on to that question, because we're going to explore it a little further later on. It's a question we need to be asking of all the 1's, 2's, 3's, 6's and 7's in the world. Our house is on fire. Why don't you care?

GOVERNMENT

The preamble to the U.S. Constitution sets forth the intentions of our Founding Fathers:

"We the People of the United States, in Order to form a more perfect Union, establish Justice, insure domestic Tranquility, provide for the common defence, promote the general Welfare, and secure the Blessings of Liberty to ourselves and our Posterity, do ordain and establish this Constitution for the United States of America."

This is what our republic is all about. We the People elect our representatives to serve our collective needs, prominently among them "to promote the general Welfare." Even in our Constitution we find the recognition of the importance of the collective We – the One Idea. Our Founders were well aware of the importance of community. Love, compassion, and empathy are a part of every healthy community. And they must be a part of any healthy government.

E pluribus unum is the phrase on the Great Seal of the United States. Translated from the Latin, it means, "Out of many, one." Here again – the One Idea.

We need each other and we need to help each other. We the People form the government to help us achieve our goals – to create healthy, satisfying, vibrant communities in which all citizens are entitled to "the blessings of liberty."

This is the mandate of the people. At all times our government should be working for the interests of all of us, for the common good, but instead we have seen the rise of what has been called "crony capitalism."

"Crony capitalism is about the aggressive and proactive use of political resources, lobbying, campaign contributions, influence-peddling of one type or another to gain something from the governmental process that wouldn't otherwise be achievable in the market. And as the time has progressed over the last two or three decades, I think it's gotten much worse. Money dominates politics." ~ David Stockman, budget director for Ronald Reagan[42]

Most of us can agree that we need to do something about the appalling corruption of our politics and our government. We desperately need principled leaders who possess genuine integrity.

"I have one yardstick by which I test every major problem – and that yardstick is: Is it good for America?"
~ Dwight D. Eisenhower[43]

We must insist that all of our representatives use that same yardstick. That is what we hire them to do, to work on behalf of the entire country, not just on behalf of one political party or the narrow interests of the extremely wealthy.

THE EXECUTIVE BRANCH

The office of the President of the United States has acquired extraordinary powers since Sept. 11, 2001.[44] The tragedy of that day has been used as an excuse to instill fear in the American people, promulgate an unnecessary war, and take away our civil liberties.

"Those who would give up essential Liberty, to purchase a little temporary Safety, deserve neither Liberty nor Safety."
~ Benjamin Franklin[45]

Though concerned citizens have been voicing concerns all along, there has been very little serious attention paid in the mainstream media.

Given all the recent changes in our laws and the rubber stamp nature of our Congress, is it now possible for any President of any political party to use his/her extraordinary powers to govern as a virtual dictatorship in America? It's a question that deserves widespread public discussion and debate.

What do *you* think?

Our votes are very important. Engaging in our democracy is important. Letting our voices be heard is important. Ultimately, We the People are responsible for our government. If we lose our democracy, we have only ourselves to blame.

CONGRESS

"Suppose you were an idiot, and suppose you were a member of Congress; but I repeat myself." ~ Mark Twain[46]

Yes, Congress is a joke. More so today than ever before.

We have a situation in which corporations and lobbyists are now writing many of the laws that govern us. Too many of our representatives don't even read or understand the legislation they vote on. Congress is so divided that members of opposite parties don't even speak to one another. Compromise has even become a dirty word.

Whatever happened to statesmanship? I can remember a time when members of Congress were held in very high regard, because they really tried to serve the best interests of their constituents, all of their constituents, not just those who belonged to their own parties.

Today, most members of Congress are so beholden to the financial entities that help them get elected, that they have lost sight of their own personal integrity. They'll say whatever they need to say and do whatever they need to do to survive in Washington. Their focus is constantly on raising more money and getting re-elected.[47] That's time that could be spent on thoroughly educating themselves about the issues, writing common-sense legislation, and advocating for what is truly in the best interests of the majority of their constituents and the country itself.

To be fair, there are still some good people in Congress with noble ideals who are trying to make a real difference. Look for them. They need your support. We need to elect more like them. They represent perhaps our best hope of restoring honesty and integrity in government.

THE JUDICIARY

"Injustice anywhere is a threat to justice everywhere."
~ Rev. Dr. Martin Luther King, Jr.[48]

The corruption of the American government is vast and pervasive. Even our judiciary has become corrupted. Corporate interests are superseding the interests of the people.

The *Citizens United* Supreme Court decision, for example, is one of the greatest travesties ever perpetrated against democracy.

"Corporations have no consciences, no beliefs, no feelings, no thoughts, no desires. Corporations help structure and facilitate the activities of human beings, to be sure, and their 'personhood' often serves as a useful legal fiction. But they are not themselves members of 'We the People' by whom and for whom our Constitution was established." ~ Justice John Paul Stevens, in his dissent for *Citizens United*

Corporations are not people and are not entitled to the same rights. Any sane person knows that, despite all the legal mumbo-jumbo proclaiming otherwise.

Through *Citizens United*, the U.S. Supreme Court handed over control of our elections to the huge corporate interests and wealthy individuals who can spend millions of dollars promoting their own preferred candidates. This under the guise of "freedom of speech." The voices of ordinary citizens, meanwhile, who can only afford to donate a few dollars here and there, are completely drowned out.

We may have made bribery legal, but it's still bribery. We should not be so naive as to think that slipping so many dollar bills into the back pockets of our politicians won't result in political favors.

"The question will arise, and arise in your day though perhaps not fully in mine: 'Which shall rule – wealth or man? Which shall lead – money or intellect? Who shall fill public stations – educated

and patriotic free men, or the feudal serfs of corporate capital?"
~ Edward G. Ryan, Chief Justice of Wisconsin, 1873[49]

Too many of our laws have been corrupted or interpreted to serve the financial needs of the elite, rather than the needs of the people themselves. Some of these laws are enabling the wanton destruction and poisoning of our environment.

So too, powerful figures in our government and in our corporate institutions have engaged in acts of wrongdoing, but are never held accountable or brought to justice.

"Ethics is knowing the difference between what you have a right to do and what is right to do." ~ Supreme Court Justice Potter Stewart

The judicial branch of our government must have great integrity. It has the considerable responsibility to fairly uphold and interpret the law. Too many judges are ideologically driven and beholden to the politicians and moneyed interests who permit them to serve on the bench. They are a disgrace to the proud tradition of American jurisprudence.

CORPORATIONS AND THE CORPORATE CULTURE

"Behind the ostensible government sits enthroned an invisible government owing no allegiance and acknowledging no responsibility to the people. To destroy this invisible government, to befoul the unholy alliance between corrupt business and corrupt politics is the first task of the statesmanship of the day."
~ Theodore Roosevelt[50]

In all that we have been discussing here in this chapter we find the corruptive influence of Big Money.

Over the course of time, corporations have become bigger and bigger and more and more powerful and less and less ethical. They were bad enough in Teddy Roosevelt's time, but today some have acquired so much power and wealth, become so huge, that they have been deemed "too big to fail." In other words, if they were to go out of business, the consequences for the global economy would be catastrophic. Businesses are interrelated and interconnected, too. It's all One.

What have we come to in our lust to satisfy our greed? These corporations are monstrosities – Frankensteins that we ourselves have created, but now they are run amok, spreading terror wherever they go.

This is not to say that all corporations are bad. Some may be involved in truly good work. What I am drawing attention to here are the worst of them, those that engage in what I would call "cutthroat corporatism." These gigantic corporations are multinational. They have no allegiance to any country or any government. They certainly don't care about the United States or any other country for that matter. They don't care how bad life in America gets for Americans who can't find jobs. They'll continue to ship their jobs overseas where they can pay slave wages to desperate workers in order to increase their already enormous profits.

They certainly don't care if people suffer or even die as a result of their ruthless business practices. And if animals go extinct, the rainforests are destroyed, the mountains are ravished, the sky, the soil, and the waters are polluted, who cares?

No matter how bad life gets in America or anywhere else in the world, the extremely wealthy who control and profit from these unethical business entities will continue to do quite well with their piles of money, buying any number of houses and yachts, corporate jets and other toys to keep them amused.

These cutthroat corporations are truly sociopathic. They are deliberately and knowingly doing very bad things to people and to the planet.

Unfortunately, we have created a system whereby a corporation's primary mission is to maximize profits. They have a legal obligation to do so. But as we have seen time and time again, these corporations do not police themselves, nor do they adhere to ethical guidelines. The system is broken. It is immoral. Most disturbingly, rarely is anyone held accountable for wrongdoing. They are literally getting away with murder.

"I believe that the officers, and, especially, the directors, of corporations should be held personally responsible when any corporation breaks the law." ~ Theodore Roosevelt[51]

There is something fundamentally wrong when businesses have a financial incentive to do harm. If we're going to save the world, we've got to do something about sociopathic corporations and the whole cutthroat business mentality.

OTHER INSTITUTIONS

So many institutions in our society have lost their way because of the corruptive influence of money – universities, churches, prisons, and hospitals, to name a few.

They are all obsessed with their own financial bottom lines. Instead of focusing on the needs of people and the community, or indeed, the needs of the planet, our institutions devote their time and energy to fiscal matters, either worrying about paying the bills or figuring out how to maximize profits.

Any institution that allows financial considerations to take precedence over the needs of the people it serves has lost sight of its true mission. We can all think of ways in which our institutions have done just that.

Even worse, so many of our institutions and businesses actually have a financial incentive to do harm to others and the planet. They make money off of the suffering of others. Every day they violate the Golden Rule.

One of the most glaring examples is our American health care system.

SPIRITUALLY AND MORALLY BANKRUPT

"A health care system should not exist to turn people into millionaires and billionaires like it does here in the United States. It should exist to make sure that everyone has access to basic health care, which is considered a human right in every other developed country in the world." ~ Thom Hartmann, radio/TV host, author[52]

Our current health care system is a huge drain on the economy. Its primary function is to make money, not to heal the sick. As such, it is spiritually and morally bankrupt.

"Americans have made healthcare a commodity when it should be primarily a human service. Healthcare cannot be left to the vagaries of the marketplace. Sickness is a universal human phenomenon that ultimately afflicts all of us. That is why economics, while important, should not drive health care. Caring for the sick, the poor, the elderly and the very young are societal obligations – not opportunities for investment and profit making." ~ Edmund Pellegrino, M.D., medical ethicist[53]

This is a system that makes money off of the suffering of people. Who benefits? The insurance companies, the health care providers, Big Business, Big Pharma. The more people who are sick and in need of services, the more money the system makes. The financial incentive is to keep people sick and using services or buying drugs. There is no financial incentive to make people healthy.[54]

"The medical profession right now is doing what? We're feasting on selling disease. And we are so successful on selling sickness that there are not enough dollars in this country to pay for it." ~ Caldwell Esselstyn, Jr., M.D., preventive medicine specialist[55]

How many millions of Americans don't seek care when they need it, because they can't afford it? How many millions of Americans are uninsured? How many millions have inadequate insurance that won't cover their medical needs when they desperately need it?

Medical costs are bankrupting far too many Americans and leaving them destitute. Think of the mental and physical agony millions and millions of patients have had to endure – thanks to the unethical, profit-mad practices of the health care industry.

Why is this acceptable, America?

"It is the responsibility of governments to enact policies that ensure the safety and well-being of a nation's people. Most industrialized nations except the United States have realized that caring for basic human needs cannot be left to the market.

Indeed, it's a mystery why U.S. corporations don't insist on a government health care program, since health care costs make U.S. companies less competitive in the global economy—while at the same time... the current U.S. system is actually more costly and less effective than those of other industrialized nations."
~ Riane Eisler, social scientist, attorney, and author[56]

If our government actually served the interests of We the People, it would fix our health care system immediately. And don't tell me this isn't possible. There are plenty of brilliant people in this country who could come up with an efficient system that is both humane and economically feasible.

The One Idea demands compassion. Access to basic human health care is a right, not a privilege to be enjoyed only by a wealthy few. If America established a single payer health care system like most of the world's industrialized countries, Americans could finally relax knowing that their health needs would be provided for. Think of the stress that would relieve! And without that stress, think how much healthier we all would be! We would not be driven by an incessant need to acquire more and more money to avert a potential financial medical catastrophe in our old age.

Fixing our health care system is not hard to do. It's just a matter of values and priorities.

THE MILITARY-INDUSTRIAL COMPLEX

"In the councils of government, we must guard against the acquisition of unwarranted influence, whether sought or unsought, by the military-industrial complex. The potential for the disastrous rise of misplaced power exists and will persist. We must never let the weight of this combination endanger our liberties or democratic processes... Only an alert and knowledge-able citizenry can compel the proper meshing of the huge industrial and military machinery of defense with our peaceful methods and goals, so that security and liberty may prosper together." ~ Dwight D. Eisenhower, 1961

President Dwight D. Eisenhower warned us about the perils of the military industrial complex in his farewell address in 1961. Since then, the aggregate of military, industrial and political interests has gained in wealth, power and influence. The intricate machinery of this conglomerate is embedded in countries, corporations, and governments around the world.

Here again we find greed at the root of the dysfunction. Corporations and unscrupulous individuals are making incredible amounts of money off of war, yet it's pretty safe to say that most of these profiteers don't get anywhere close to exposing themselves to the dangers and horrors of war that they are largely responsible for creating.

Society pays a steep price when its resources are devoted to making war, rather than to securing and maintaining peace. We have reached a point in the evolution of humankind where war is no longer a viable option. Progress will only be made with diplomacy, humanitarian outreach and an understanding of our global interdependence on one another.

"According to World Military & Social Expenditures, the cost of a U.S. intercontinental ballistic missile would feed 50 million children, build 160,000 schools, or open 340,000 health centers."
~ Riane Eisler[57]

War itself is psychosis. It is the worst disease that afflicts the soul of humankind. It represents the complete and total breakdown of societal health.

"All war is a symptom of man's failure as a thinking animal."
~ John Steinbeck[58]

The warmongers have a financial incentive to promote death and destruction. They will do their best through their instruments of propaganda in the media and elsewhere to create conflict and try to make us fear and hate one another, often in the guise of extreme nationalism or overblown patriotism.

The truth? Only love and courage will make this world a safer place. Hatred and fear will make it more dangerous.

The Iranian Girl

There's a hole in the ground
A moving of earth, now made
A sad depression
Where once she played in
Puddle-rain
Splashing with the joy that comes
From child-like feet

The sound is still here
In the air, the breeze yet carrying
The secret laughter
That haunts the waking hours of those
Who've lost the way

How vain to think that
Memory can be erased

All will remember
No one escapes

"The world has achieved brilliance without wisdom, power without conscience. Ours is a world of nuclear giants and ethical infants. We know more about war than we know about peace, we know more about killing than we know about living."
~ Gen. Omar Bradley[59]

"Never think that war, no matter how necessary, nor how justified, is not a crime." ~ Ernest Hemingway

"Humanity should question itself, once more, about the absurd and always unfair phenomenon of war, on whose stage of death and pain only remains standing the negotiating table that could and should have prevented it." ~ Pope John Paul II

I wonder if she saw it
The moment before
Her hair still flying free
The metal catching that last
Pure glint of sun

Did she hear the explosion
That made no sense
Did she feel
Her body come apart
And fall like dust, too soon

Does anyone ask
Whatever she felt, whatever she dreamed
Her dreaming time is gone
And no lofty word of God or
Glory will ever make it right

Dare to listen and you will
Hear her
Dare to open your eyes and see

The Iranian girl
No different
Like you, like me.

With the death of a single man, woman, or child, war slays a host of generations who might otherwise have thrived in a peaceful world. Here in the 21st century, we need to reasonably address our differences through diplomatic channels. Maturity is required of us all.

Only peace will take us where we need to go.

"There was never a good war, or a bad peace." ~ Benjamin Franklin, 1783[60]

THE BANKS, WALL STREET, AND OTHER FINANCIAL INSTITUTIONS

The Big Banks, Wall Street, and other financial institutions make all of our commerce – both ethical and unethical – possible. They drive the economic engines of the world and bear a considerable responsibility for fanning the flames of our burning house.

It used to be that gambling was considered a vice, because of its enormous social costs. Apparently that has changed in recent decades. Gambling has become socially acceptable. Americans now have access to gambling casinos in most states.

That doesn't change the reality. Like alcohol and drugs, gambling can be a very addictive behavior. People's lives are destroyed because of it.

"In a bet there is a fool and a thief." ~ Proverb

The people who work in financial industries have become the ultimate game-players. They have created what has truly become one big international gambling casino. Theirs is not a world that cares about conscience or social responsibility or economic justice. And yet, these are the very people who are running the world. Does that make any sense?

How much responsibility do these institutions and their CEO's, their boards, their shareholders, and their employees bear for all the lives that have been ruined?

It is time to hold our financial institutions accountable for actions that contribute to the destruction of people and the planet. The power of these institutions must be checked by strong government oversight and regulations to serve the common good. And when I say "government" here, I mean true democratic government – of, by, and for the people – not corrupted government – of, by, and for the corporations and the extremely wealthy. A corrupted government will only continue to feed the destructive status quo and allow the free-for-all financial gambling operations to continue.

WHO ARE THE 6's AND 7's?

We've talked about the 1's, 2's and 3's. The 1's are in the dark. They haven't a clue about what's going on. They don't even know that the house is on fire. The 2's know it's on fire, but are indifferent, too lazy, too cynical, or too selfish to bother to get involved. The 3's can see what's happening, but are petrified, not knowing what to do to help or how to do it.

The 4's and 5's are the heroes of this drama. They know the house is on fire and are determined to put it out. The 5's are even willing to risk their lives to save the lives of others.

But who are the 6's and 7's?

In many cases the 7's, the most egregious abusers of others, aren't human beings at all. They are, as we have seen, the systems and institutions we have created. Their activities are criminal in many respects. At some point in the not-so-distant future, when people awaken to the truth of what has been happening, these rogue entities and the people involved in them may even be held accountable for "crimes against humanity."

There are, of course, individual persons who are also number 7's. Psychologists would probably call them sociopathic or psychopathic. They are spiritually and/or mentally ill. They may be very powerful people, very wealthy people – or not – they may be people in your community who seem quite ordinary.

No matter what roles they may play in this world, the 7's are people without conscience. They act selfishly without genuine concern for their fellow human beings. They knowingly and deliberately hurt others.

"Power tends to corrupt and absolute power corrupts absolutely."
~ Sir John Dalberg-Acton, historian[61]

Now how about the 6's? Who are they?

The 6's are all those people who are aiding and abetting the 7's and in some way profiting from the burning down of the house. They may work for corporations and other institutions that are hurting others, but they turn a blind eye to the negative consequences of their actions. They have rationalized their station in life: That's business. What can you do? I have to make a living. I have to feed my family. That's the way life is. You can't fight it, can you?

How many 6's are out there? Way too many. Too many people are compromising their own integrity, their own humanity, in order to accommodate the unscrupulous or unethical practices that their jobs demand. But while the 7's may be so ill that they are difficult to reach, the 6's are not hopelessly lost. Most still have a conscience and a good heart in there somewhere. We have to convince them to change their ways and join us.

THE MOB MENTALITY

We all know what happens when people become part of a mob. The mob starts to get out of control. Emotion takes over from reason. People misbehave. They do things they would never do as individuals. When they see others doing something wrong they say, "well if they can do that, I can do that too, and get away with it!" The worst parts of themselves come to the fore and are given malignant expression.

People can easily become 6's and 7's when they are part of a mob, because no one is there to hold them accountable. They can hide behind a sea of human anonymity and no one will ever know they were a part of it.

The same is true in the corporate world. People can hide behind a corporation and never be held accountable as an individual for engaging in wrongdoing. They'll do whatever the corporation wants them to do. They may do things on their jobs that they would never dream of doing if their friends and neighbors knew they were doing it. But with a huge corporation to hide behind? And getting paid lots of money for it? They'll do whatever it takes to turn that profit and no one will ever be the wiser.

The mob mentality is, after all, the refuge of cowards. There is nothing noble about submitting to the unconscionable will of those who treat us with callous disregard. It is courage that we admire. The courage to stand up for what is right.

The old profit-driven Bottom Line has done too much damage to too many lives. The new Bottom Line is humanity itself. Those who advocate profit over principle will find themselves increasingly out-of-touch with their fellow Americans and people of good will all over the world as the 21st century continues to unfold.

THE BETTER ANGELS

"Please make it fashionable to be compassionate."
~ Archbishop Desmond Tutu[62]

If we are to truly save the world, we must commit to the One Idea. We must appeal to the good in people. We must appeal to their consciences, what Abraham Lincoln called, "the better angels of our nature."[63]

The corporate value system in which making money takes precedence over the welfare of human beings and the planet is not sustainable. It is corrupt. It is immoral. It must change.

These corporate multinationals are leading us like the Pied Piper of Hamelin to our own self-destruction. We have been mesmerized by the music, bewitched by the baubles dangled in front of our eyes, but it's time to wake up.

"Only when the last tree is cut, only when the last river is polluted, only when the last fish is caught, will they realize that you can't eat money." ~ Native American proverb

The obsession with accumulating exorbitant amounts of money and power must end. The Age of Selfishness and Greed is over.

"It is easier for a camel to go through the eye of a needle, than for a rich man to enter into the kingdom of God." ~ Mark, 10:25

The Age of Kindness and Generosity is underway. Our spiritually ill value system is being replaced by a healthy, compassionate one. This is our next great challenge in the course of human spiritual evolution. We must acknowledge that we are part of a whole and learn to cherish and respect all the individual parts of the whole. All is One. We are One.

"You must work, we must all work, to make the world worthy of its children." ~ Pablo Casals, cellist and conductor

Only through love will we find our way to create a world worthy of our children and grandchildren.

It's one thing to talk about how our institutions are contributing to the destruction of the world and our quality of life, but as individuals most of us seemingly have little control over what these huge institutions do.

In the next chapter, we'll take a look at some of the things each one of us can do, every day, to douse the flames that are threatening us all.

CHAPTER FIVE

Dousing
the Flames

CHAPTER FIVE

Dousing the Flames

In the previous chapters, we talked about why the world – our house – is on fire, focusing in particular on the negative roles that our institutions play. Let's remember, however, that institutions are made of individual people, people like you and me.

If most of the people within an institution commit to being ethical and doing the right thing themselves, then that institution will fundamentally change. Of course, the people in positions of authority bear an even greater responsibility. They must set ethical standards and guidelines and lead by example.

So you see, change begins with each of us. We can reform our institutions, our systems, and transform them into true reflections of our best selves. We can no longer afford to turn a blind eye to misbehaviors. We must encourage our institutions and the leadership at the top to become 4's and 5's, not 6's and 7's.

In the last chapter we talked about religion, politics, the media, government, corporations, etc. All of us have a role to play in all of these institutions. Let's look at them again, but this time let's focus on what each of us can do to help douse the flames.

Are you ready? Grab a bucket.

Bucket #1: Religion

When it comes to religion and spiritual beliefs, do you have an open mind and an open heart? Do you care about everyone or do you harbor resentments and hatreds for other people because of their religious (or non-religious) beliefs? Are you self-righteous and judgmental or are you understanding and forgiving?

If you belong to a church, what role do you play within that church? Are you working to bring people together with compassion or are you working to separate and divide people? Are you working for the good of all people on the planet?

What kind of personal example do you set as a religious person? Are you loving and kind to everyone? Remember, all of the major faiths promote some version of The Golden Rule.

"Inherent in religion, at its best, is a commitment to doing good in the world." ~ Karen Armstrong[64]

We all know that, throughout history, organized religions and the people involved with them have been responsible for a good deal of pain and suffering in the world. When they have gone wrong, they have forgotten the truth of their own message – The Golden Rule. Nothing is more galling than the hypocrisy of religious people who, in the name of doing good, are actually doing harm.

But let's be fair. Religious communities have also been involved in a lot of honorable and heroic work. They often come to the aid of those in need when no one else will. Billions of people all over the world have benefitted from their positive relationships with religious organizations. This is a good thing. Let's give credit where credit is due.

We are now living in an era when, as a global community, we must strongly encourage organized religions to be what they are intended to be: forces for good, for kindness, for love and compassion.

Religions and religious people must be among the 4's and 5's who help to put out the fire. Religious leaders can have a profound impact in this regard, because they have perhaps more power and influence than governments or any other institutions. They must live up to their spiritual and ethical responsibilities.

Violent religious extremism is never acceptable. Whenever religious leaders or their followers promote a negative message, working to divide us, fomenting hatred rather than trying to bring us together, we should let them know that that sort of reprehensible behavior is anathema to us all. In so doing, we will also send a message to our children that hatred has no place in a civilized society.

THE GOD QUESTION

"The fool doth think he is wise, but the wise man knows himself to be a fool." ~ William Shakespeare[65]

"He who thinks he knows, doesn't know. He who knows that he doesn't know, knows." ~ Joseph Campbell[66]

Okay, now we get to the real nitty gritty: The God Question. Is there a God or isn't there? There are a lot of people out there who insist on being right about this issue, no matter which side they come down on. Their intransigence, their fanaticism, their extremism is the cause of a lot of suffering in this world and has led to great conflict, even war.

Moreover, we can't even agree on who or what God is. Everyone has his or her own ideas. Is God a being, a person, an energy, a force? Is God loving, cruel, or indifferent? External or internal, active or passive, knowable or unknowable? When we talk about God, we don't even know if we're talking about the same thing!

The truth is no one knows. You cannot prove the existence of God, nor can you disprove it. We live in a mystery. We can only have FAITH in what we believe to be true. But if we are wise, if we have a kind heart, we will always be ready to admit that we could be wrong. We are only human, after all. We don't know everything. The Universe may well be something quite different than we believe it to be.

The healthiest approach is to allow every individual the freedom to believe whatever he/she chooses to believe. This is freedom of conscience, a fundamental human right.

Besides, what is really important is not what we believe to be true in our heads, but what we know to be true in our hearts: love. We need to care about all human beings, all life on the planet, and the planet itself. That's where we have to agree.

"More and more, I think God is the name we give to our sense that everything is connected to everything else."
~ Rabbi Lawrence Kushner[67]

We all have choices to make within the limits of our knowledge and the dictates of our conscience. Those choices will differ from individual to individual and from culture to culture. Let's allow that to be okay.

Besides, whenever we are annoyed and frustrated by the beliefs and behaviors of others, we might take it as an opportunity to learn more about ourselves.

"Everything that irritates us about others can lead us to an understanding about ourselves." ~ Carl Jung[68]

"When you see a good man, think of emulating him; when you see a bad man, examine your heart." ~ Chinese Proverb

Here are some suggestions that each of us can do that would help us all to have better relations.

- Live with an open mind and an open heart.
- Always choose love over fear and kindness over cruelty.
- Be willing to learn and to grow.

Let's be open to increasing our knowledge and understanding of others and the world. Let's be sensitive to those who may disagree with us and willing to listen to what they have to say. So often, those who are close-minded, those who refuse to listen or entertain new ideas are often the same people who close their hearts as well, who treat others with disdain, even hatred.

"Every religion is good that teaches man to be good; and I know of none that instructs him to be bad." ~ Thomas Paine[69]

A well-rounded person should be open to both science and spirituality. One without the other, it seems to me, is insufficient to appreciating and understanding our place in the Universe.

THE SEPARATION OF CHURCH AND STATE

"Religious factions will go on imposing their will on others unless the decent people connected to them recognize that religion has no place in public policy. They must learn to make their views known without trying to make their views the only alternatives."
~ Barry Goldwater[70]

As I said before, freedom of conscience is a fundamental human right. No one can truly be free if they don't have the ability to believe and worship (or not) as they choose.

In the U.S., the principle of the separation of church and state has served us well.

"We establish no religion in this country, we command no worship, we mandate no belief, nor will we ever. Church and state are, and must remain, separate." ~ Ronald Reagan[71]

Disturbingly, however, in America today, there are fanatical factions of religious "believers" who are trying to undermine the time-honored principle of the separation of church and state. It seems, if they had their way, they would establish what would amount to a theocracy in America, imposing their views on everyone else. Every American ought to be appalled by such intolerant and blatantly anti-democratic movements.

The separation of church and state protects people of all faiths and no faith. No religion should be able to exercise control over a government and thereby dictate its theology onto any diverse group of free people.

"We all agree that neither the Government nor political parties ought to interfere with religious sects. It is equally true that religious sects ought not to interfere with the Government or with political parties. We believe that the cause of good government and the cause of religion suffer by all such interference." ~ Rutherford B. Hayes[72]

BUCKET #2: POLITICS, POLITICIANS AND POLITICAL PARTIES

Our politics are a mess, right? We all know that.

Money has completely corrupted our political process. We need to get the money out of politics. Politicians and political parties should be accountable to We the People. They should not be beholden to lobbyists and corporate entities whose only agenda is to increase profits for their narrow selfish interests.

What can you do to help put out the flames?

- Support efforts to get the money out of politics, including those to overturn *Citizens United.*

- When you find a candidate for any political office that you trust and believe in, go the extra mile and work to help get her/him elected.
- Think independently. Even if you belong to a political party, remember you are a human being first. Don't succumb to the team mentality that refuses to listen to, or even consider, opposing points of view. Remember, good politics requires knowing the facts, using common sense, and finding compromise.
- Run for political office yourself and set a standard for leadership with integrity.

These are just a few suggestions. You will undoubtedly be able to think of many more ways to help.

Government of the corporations, by the corporations and for the corporations is destroying our nation. The shifting of power upwards to the extremely wealthy has got to stop. It's not fair. It's not democracy.

"An imbalance between rich and poor is the oldest and most fatal ailment of all republics." ~ Plutarch, Greek historian (c. 46-120 CE)

If we can get the money out of politics, we will drastically reduce corruption and, in fact, we will be doing all of our politicians, as well as ourselves, a huge favor. Politicians are human. Believe it or not, they have families and children, too. They would love to be able to look in the mirror and see someone that they can respect, someone who believes he or she is doing the right thing and improving the lives of most Americans. They would much rather spend their time working on issues for the common good of the country, instead of bending to the will of wealthy corporate interests, kissing lobbyists' derrieres and raising mountains of cash just to get re-elected.

Our politicians are prisoners of a profoundly corrupt system. Imagine yourself trying to survive politically in such a dark, dysfunctional world.

We need to free them. Let's get the money out of politics and return our government to the people.

BUCKET #3: THE MEDIA

As we discussed in the last chapter, our corporate mainstream news media are largely responsible for the sorry state of our world. They have become the mouthpiece for the greedy corporate profit-making agenda. If these media were focused on telling the truth, we would not have a problem with so many people remaining in denial of the climate science and we could summon the political will to effect the necessary change.

Instead of helping us to douse the flames, however, too often the media are fanning them. They ought to be seeking out the truth of what's happening on this planet and delivering the important news in an objective manner. They ought to be fostering real discussion and debate. Instead, they subject us to a plethora of biased pundits who make their money by grinding their political axes, when what we really need are nonpartisan, knowledgeable people who are working to confront the issues through the dissemination of factual information.

How much time do we spend watching TV, anyway? Or talking or texting on cell phones, or dithering about aimlessly on the computer? Most of us can admit we could probably find better uses for our time. There are other ways to entertain ourselves that would be much more beneficial to our lives and the lives of others: reading, writing, drawing, painting, gardening, exercising, meeting with friends, etc. Better yet, what if we took a little time each day working in some way to save the world? Now there's an idea whose time has come.

Here are just a few suggestions for how you can aim your buckets at the media to help put out the flames.

- Avoid watching TV programs or movies that aren't in some way enriching your life.
- Avoid news programs that aren't telling you the truth. Deliberately slanting the news or spewing misinformation to promote a political agenda is unacceptable.
- Don't allow your children to watch programs or movies, or play video games, that are unhealthy for them, psychologically or spiritually, particularly violent, mean-spirited programs that

violate the One Idea. Also, be sure to share your concerns honestly with them.

- Demand more educational programming.
- Don't buy products from sponsors of programs that you find objectionable. Your dollars only encourage their poor behavior.
- Write letters, sign petitions, make phone calls and let media know when you object to their programming or practices.
- Support news outlets that tell the truth, do investigative reporting, and employ respectable, dedicated journalists with integrity. These people are among the 4's and 5's who serve the public good.
- Support organizations that hold media accountable for their practices.

Remember, these media are dependent upon your support. If you don't like what they are offering, let them know. Withdraw your financial support and tell them why. This is very important. They contend they are giving us what we want. Really? I don't believe most Americans are so vapid, do you? Media shouldn't insult our intelligence. Let's let them know in no uncertain terms that we are not happy with their output. We want truthful media that are going to be beneficial to our society, not harmful to it.

BUCKET #4: GOVERNMENT

Let's always remember that our Founders gave us a republic, a representative democracy, but nothing is guaranteed to last forever. We have to work to preserve and improve it.

In order for this democracy to work, We the People must get involved. We must be responsible citizens and demand integrity from our leaders. Unfortunately, most Americans really aren't paying much attention to what's going on with their government. That's a tragedy, because our democracy is quickly slipping away. The powerful, the wealthy, the corporations, the 6's and 7's have taken over. They make up fewer than 1% of us and are living high off the hog and having a great time at the expense of everyone else. The rest of us, more than 99% of us, aren't really represented by our politicians or our government. Our interests are being ignored. Why? Because our interests are opposed to the selfish interests of the 6's and 7's who just want to increase their profits. They really don't care about the quality of life of the vast majority of Americans.

To provide employment, education, health, and safety for all Americans requires money. That's money the 6's and 7's don't want to spend on us. They prefer to keep it for themselves and that's exactly what they've been doing for decades, always finding new ways to further line their own pockets while shoving financial burdens onto everyone else. Greed has no end. It is addictive and obsessive.

"Democracy doesn't begin at the top; it begins at the bottom when flesh and blood human beings rekindle the patriot's dream." ~ Bill Moyers[73]

What can we do? To reclaim our government, all of us ordinary people must get active. It's going to take an awful lot of our buckets to put out this fire! Here are some suggestions:

- Inform yourself about what is actually going on. It will take some time and effort to get to the truth. Don't limit yourself to the mainstream news media. Read many different sources of information on the Internet and elsewhere. There are also many excellent film documentaries that are focusing attention on extremely important issues. See Appendix A for some recommended viewing.

- Support efforts to inform and educate the American people. To this end, Government, Civics, and American History should be taught in our schools.

- Vote. Voting is the very least we can do. Vote every single chance you get in every single election. We need to elect leaders with integrity on all levels, local, state and national. Be sure to vote also on the many important ballot measures that can affect your life in positive and/or negative ways. When making up our minds in determining how to vote, we should consider the impacts of our choices on the lives of not only ourselves, but also our fellow citizens, future generations, and the entire global community.

- Demand that the vote be legitimate. Electronic voting machines are too easily hacked and results manipulated. Votes should have verifiable paper trails. Without them, citizens can have no confidence that the voting results are accurate. If we can't trust the vote, our democracy is not a real democracy, it is only the illusion of democracy.
- Support organizations that are working for honest elections and verifiable voting methods.
- Write letters, sign petitions, make phone calls to your representatives and let them know your thoughts and feelings often and repeatedly. This is your democracy. Take responsibility for doing your part.
- Organize. Meet with others to discuss issues that are important to you and explore ways to take action.
- Demonstrate against wrongdoing and injustice. Organized demonstrations by concerned citizens are among the most effective tools to promote change. Marching in the streets, sit-ins and other forms of peaceful protest can draw attention to serious issues. Always practice nonviolence in these situations. More on this later.
- Demand statesmanship from our politicians. They are our leaders. They set an example for us all. They ought to be working together to do what's in the best interests of the people and the nation. Hold them accountable when they conduct themselves dishonorably.

Every day try to throw at least one bucket of water on the fire – write a letter, sign a petition – DO something. We must not succumb to defeatism or despair.

> "...once we decide that we're powerless, our passivity becomes a self-fulfilling prophecy, a habit of mind that's harder and harder to shake. We decide we can do nothing about key common issues, large or small. Then we withdraw from public life before giving it a serious shot. If enough of us withdraw, we hand power over to the greediest." ~ Paul Loeb, author[74]

We are not powerless. We still have the power to change what's happening in this country if we all do our part. The worst thing anyone can do is nothing.

"The world is in greater peril from those who tolerate or encourage evil than from those who actually commit it."
~ Albert Einstein[75]

Don't listen to the naysayers and the defeatists who moan and complain about the house burning down, but don't do a thing to help put it out. They are among the 2's who think they know everything and have convinced themselves that there is no hope. Nothing could be further from the truth. There is always hope when people take a stand for what is right.

Did you know that conventional wisdom says that one phone call to a legislator is equivalent to one hundred constituents' voices and one letter is equal to one thousand? When you write a letter to your senators or members of Congress, you're actually representing 1,000 of your peers. That's power.

As for petitions, they represent the voices of citizens taking a stand and speaking out against wrongdoing and injustice. That is never a waste of time, no matter what the result. Moreover, in my experience, as someone who signs petitions on a regular basis, I continually see positive results from our efforts. Don't believe those who say it doesn't do any good. It's simply not true.

If you want real change, you've got to help. Don't expect others to make your life better if you aren't willing to lift a finger. That just isn't fair to all the 4's and 5's who are on the front lines, fighting the fires.

Apathy is the slow poison coursing through the body politic that paves the way to tyranny.

Too many Americans think that voting is all they need to do, as if electing a certain candidate will somehow right all the wrongs in our society. Then they get all upset when they don't see any real change, when all the promises their candidate made are not realized. Politicians can't snap their fingers and change everything. As I said, they are prisoners of a very corrupt system. The moneyed interests are extremely powerful and aren't about to give in.

Voting is the least we can do, yet many Americans don't even care enough to do that! There will be no real change until millions of people stand up to demand it. History has shown over and over again that progress will be slow and painstakingly difficult.

Every day Americans need to advocate for what they believe in. They need to push and prod their representatives and constantly urge them to do the right thing.

Imagine if hundreds of thousands, even millions of people made their voices heard on any issue. Do you think our government officials would finally listen? Of course they would. They'd have to. Their jobs are in jeopardy. We still have the ability to fire them come the next election.

"As long as the world shall last, there will be wrongs, and if no man objected and no man rebelled, those wrongs would last forever." ~ Clarence Darrow[76]

Get involved. Fight back. The more that We the People express our outrage, the better the opportunity for real change.

THE IMPORTANCE OF NONVIOLENCE

A very important point must be made here. Fighting back does not mean resorting to violence. Violence is never acceptable as a means for political protest and change. Violence is diametrically opposed to the One Idea. When we harm others, we only hurt ourselves.

"If you and I are having a single thought of violence or hatred against anyone in the world at this moment, we are contributing to the wounding of the world." ~ Deepak Chopra[77]

Any social movement that resorts to violence and the harming of innocent people in order to spread its message will quickly lose credibility, as well as the support of good people everywhere. After all, it is hypocritical to demand social justice for the weak and oppressed, while at the same time employing the same violent tactics used by the oppressors.

"Hate begets hate; violence begets violence; toughness begets a greater toughness. We must meet the forces of hate with the power of love." ~ Rev. Dr. Martin Luther King, Jr.[78]

Protests must always be peaceful, even in the face of savage opposition by the police and military forces of the state. Answering violence with violence only creates more violence. The movements of Gandhi, King and many others have shown us how effective nonviolent protest can be. Keeping the One Idea in mind, we remember that we are acting out of love – for the good of all, including those who oppose us. The police, after all, are our friends and neighbors.

"Whenever you have truth it must be given with love, or the message and the messenger will be rejected." ~ Mahatma Gandhi

One of the most iconic images that exemplifies delivering the message with love is the photograph of a young Vietnam War protestor placing a flower in the barrel of a National Guardsman's rifle.[79]

Organizers of protests must insist upon nonviolence from all participants. If people can't control their anger, they ought to stay home. Screaming obscenities at the police is counterproductive and will never win the hearts and minds of one's fellow citizens. Moreover, such behavior puts one's fellow protestors at risk. Violent confrontation only leads to pain and suffering and sometimes death.

The job of the police is to maintain the peace, to protect all citizens from harm. At least, that's what their job *should* be in a free and open democracy. But too often what we see is police bullying. The state's intent, through their police and military forces, is made clear by their actions: to intimidate and silence the opposition through show of force and aggressive, often violent, tactics. That's what bullies do. Who are they really protecting? Let's face it. They are protecting the interests of those who are in power, many of whom are 6's and 7's.

The police should not be resorting to violence themselves. Those officers who are 4's and 5's know it and are disgusted by it. Oh yes, let's not forget, many of our policemen and -women are real heroes. Their acts of heroism are documented every day. They have a tough job. They know that the use of brutal, inhumane tactics against unarmed, peaceful protestors is not only completely out of line, it is also cowardly and shameful.

The more that protestors can be creative in delivering their messages with love, the more successful they will be. Why? Because the public will quickly recognize the stark contrast between right and wrong, between love and injustice, between peaceful protestors and bullying police officers.

Remember, winning the hearts and minds of the populace is what this is all about, creating the momentum to effect positive political change in the halls of government.

Protestors must have faith that, ultimately, truth, love, and justice will win the day.

"I believe that unarmed truth and unconditional love will have the final word in reality. This is why right, temporarily defeated, is stronger than evil triumphant." ~ Rev. Dr. Martin Luther King, Jr.[80]

There are many ways to deliver a peaceful message. Some have found silent protests to be very effective. Others have focused on making the protests educational experiences, informing the public about the issues involved. Some have made their protests family-friendly, bringing their kids and providing music and entertainment. When children are present, the police have an even greater responsibility to show restraint and maintain the peace.

Protesting against injustice is part of our revolutionary American heritage and legacy. It is a right guaranteed by the First Amendment.

"Congress shall make no law respecting an establishment of religion, or prohibiting the free exercise thereof; or abridging the freedom of speech, or of the press; or the right of the people peaceably to assemble, and to petition the Government for a redress of grievances." ~ The First Amendment to the United States Constitution

Where would our country be today without the organized protests of so many brave and conscientious citizens against the injustices of our society in times past? These people are number 5's. They risk their lives for truth and justice. We are indebted to them all. Without their efforts, we might still be living in a time when women didn't have the right to vote, when workers didn't have the right to organize, and when African Americans had virtually no equal protections under the law.

Even today, women, workers and African Americans are still struggling mightily against the entrenched forces, who in their lust for power and wealth, would strip them of their rights and their dignity.

All Americans should support the right of their fellow citizens to engage in peaceful protest and be proud that we live in a country where citizens still have that right.

As I write this, however, more and more laws are being passed to restrict the free speech rights of American citizens. We are seeing the rise of a militarized police state that is aggressively and often violently cracking down on peaceful protesters. This is yet another frightening development for those who love freedom and democracy.

Bucket #5: Corporations and the Corporate Culture

"The fact of the matter is that today, stuff-selling mega-corporations have a huge influence on our daily lives. And because of the competitive nature of our global economy, these corporations are generally only concerned with one thing... the bottom line. That is, maximizing profit, regardless of the social or environmental costs." ~ David Suzuki[81]

Most small businesses begin with fairly pure motives – to perform services or offer products that will be of benefit and use to others, and in the process, make a profit. Small business owners are responsive to the concerns and needs of their customers in their communities. Their customers are their neighbors, after all. If they don't pay attention to them, they will lose their trust and their patronage and the business will fail.

Small business owners are personally invested in their businesses. They want them to be a credit to themselves and their communities. They want to take pride in what they do. They recognize the need to treat their employees, as well as their customers, decently and fairly. Small businesses become like families. In healthy businesses, as in healthy families, everyone truly cares about one another and all are working to make the business a success.

This small business model works. It works very well. Small businesses have served our communities and our country with distinction across the generations.

But in modern times, many small businesses have been swallowed up by much larger corporate entities. As these corporations become larger and larger, they become less and less humane and more and more sociopathic. They also become less democratic and more authoritarian. Ultimately, all they really care about is making more and more money and they don't care how they do it.

Big Fish, Small Pond

The corporation got so big
Swallowing little corporation
After little corporation
It finally swallowed—Itself.

The destruction was so vast
So completely global
It was impossible to figure out
Who to blame.

Now we are at the point that the entire world is basically being run by these multinational, sociopathic, authoritarian entities we call corporations and all of us are suffering for it.

There should be no such thing as a business that is "too big to fail." If it's that big, we need to take steps to break up that company into smaller units. We should not find ourselves in a position that the fate of the world is dependent on a corporation's survival at all costs.

"A business that makes nothing but money is a poor business."
~ Henry Ford[82]

Any business that cannot make an honest profit, or pay its employees a livable wage or provide for their safety, does not deserve to be in business. Nor do companies that do not behave in ethical and socially responsible ways. Yet, how many corporations are now failing that test?

"Corporation, n. An ingenious device for obtaining individual profit without individual responsibility." ~ Ambrose Bierce[83]

Here are some suggestions for how you as an individual can aim your buckets of water at the unethical, cutthroat corporations in our midst.

- Educate yourself. Find out how various corporations are doing business.
- Do not do business with companies whose practices are detrimental to their workers or our communities. Take your business to more responsible companies instead. Support small, local businesses as much as possible.
- Encourage companies to do the right thing. Send them letters, make phone calls, etc. to make your voice heard.
- If you are a shareholder, demand ethical business practices from those companies in which you invest.
- Support organizations that are holding companies accountable for their unethical and sometimes criminal behavior.
- End corporate welfare. Oppose the use of your tax dollars to subsidize already hugely profitable corporations, especially those that are causing harm to others and/or the environment.

Generally speaking, the corporate culture is very unhealthy. No one likes authoritarianism, except those who wield the power. Corporations demand a kind of blind obedience from their employees. People have to toe a very strict line and don't feel free to be themselves. Often they are not treated with respect by their superiors, nor are they paid fairly for the difficult work they do.

When a corporation is looking to cut corners, the first place they go is the employees, cutting jobs, salaries and benefits. A small business owner, on the other hand, who cares about his/her employees is going to look for other ways to cut costs.

Every individual in a corporation, even the top brass, is completely expendable. The corporation couldn't care less about them as human beings. Everyone is simply a cog in a vast profit-making machine, but those profits are too often not shared equitably with the workers who actually do the essential work that keeps the corporation in business. In fact, too often we see the corporate bigwigs taking humongous salaries and bonuses, while at the same time hundreds, even thousands, of hapless, powerless employees are given the pink slip.

Historically, unions have provided workers with the best defense against widespread corporate abuse. Unions have given workers a voice and allowed them to bargain for fair wages and safe working conditions. They have been a key factor in raising the standard of living for the entire middle class, not just for union members.[84] It is not surprising then that unions have been viciously targeted by the corporate sector and their power has been substantially diminished over the last few decades.

It ought to be abundantly clear to all fair-minded people that workers must have rights, especially the right to collective bargaining. Employees deserve to be treated fairly, with dignity and respect. Our laws must protect them from exploitation and abuse.

More and more people are recognizing that the cutthroat corporate culture isn't working. It is devoid of humanity, and as such, is in violation of the One Idea. These corporations do not abide by any Golden Rule.

The corporate environment creates resentment that kills morale and can cast a deathly pall over the workplace. This negative energy bleeds out into the rest of society causing unhappiness and unrest.

It does not have to be this way. We can change the corporate culture if we demand change.

Most people spend far more time at work than they do with their families or their friends. I think it's fair to say that many people, especially if they work for a huge corporation, don't even particularly enjoy their jobs. Too many actually hate their jobs. How unhealthy is that? Life is too short, isn't it, to waste in jobs that don't fulfill us in some way? What is the spiritual and emotional cost of waking up every day and loathing going to work?

Life is a precious gift. Each of us has only a short time available to us.

The societal anxiety and depression that is created by our unhealthy work environments exacts a terrible price. People become nasty, mean, and irritable. They may become quick to anger and lash out in inappropriate ways. We all see these negative behaviors every day. Is it any wonder so few of us are able to live by the Golden Rule when we are treated so disrespectfully on our jobs? And how many of us take out our frustrations on our spouses and kids?

In a healthy world, we have safe, respectful work environments where every employee is valued as a human being, paid fairly, and treated with dignity. In such an atmosphere people enjoy each other's company, they work amiably together to ensure the company's success, because each of them has a personal stake in it. They wake up every day feeling good about going to work, because on some deep meaningful level they enjoy it. Their work makes them feel good – about themselves and others.

How about you? Are you genuinely enjoying your work in some way? Is your work meaningful? The greatest satisfaction comes from giving, not taking. Are you giving back to your community? If you're not here to make this world a better place, then why are you here?

"Generosity is giving more than you can, and pride is taking less than you need." ~ Kahlil Gibran

BEWARE OF SHEEP'S CLOTHING

"...one may smile, and smile, and be a villain..."
~ William Shakespeare[85]

The sociopathic corporations that are deliberately involved in harmful practices against humanity and the planet have a ton of money that they can spend to distort the truth and manipulate public opinion. Every day we see commercials on TV that tell us how wonderful they are. Often, they will make claims that directly contradict the transgressions of which they are accused. They really have no shame. They are like the bully on the school playground who pushes the other kids around and then complains to the teacher about how all the kids are picking on him. Our inept media, in the meantime, do not expose the duplicity of these corporate villains.

As the public moves into growing awareness, these Machiavellian corporate ne'er-do-wells will quadruple their efforts to dupe the public. We must all be on our guard to seek out the truth and demand accountability.

ETHICAL CORPORATIONS: THE WAVE OF THE FUTURE?

As a society we need to seriously debate the roles that corporations should play as we move to a sustainable world. The modern-day cutthroat corporate model that places the making of money above all else doesn't work and is doing great harm.

There are other ways of doing business. The small business model, as I've said before, is a good one. The question is: how can a corporation maintain its "humanity" as it grows bigger and bigger?

No matter how we approach the problem, we must remember that it is always within our power to insist on ethical business practices that are responsive to human beings and the environment. Corporations are created by government permission. We can limit their monopolistic powers, curb abuse, and ensure accountability.

And I ask you, what kind-hearted, sensible person wouldn't want that?

Have you ever heard of B Corporations? The B stands for benefit. These are corporations that make it a part of their business model to do good for the environment and their communities. They are socially and environmentally conscious entities. At present, they are certified by B Lab, a non-profit organization. To qualify they must meet performance and legal accountability standards. As I write this there are 552 Certified B Corporations that encompass 60 different industries.[86]

Imagine if all corporations behaved ethically and paid serious attention to the social and environmental needs of our communities. What a different world this would be, wouldn't it?

"Our human destiny is inextricably linked to the actions of all other living beings. Respecting this principle is the fundamental challenge in changing the nature of business." ~ Paul Hawken[87]

Our economic system, our way of doing business, is bound to change over time as we meet the challenges that lie in front of us. As our system evolves, it is essential to incorporate the essence of the One Idea – love, compassion, and the Golden Rule.

BUCKET #6: OTHER INSTITUTIONS

As we move further into the 21st century, we need to demand that all of our institutions – schools, universities, hospitals, prisons, etc. – put people and the planet over profits.

You may have noticed I've been using the word "demand" quite a bit. It's a strong word. It's decisive. There's nothing wimpy about it. We have to get active, folks. The times *demand* it.

Those of us who are a part of these institutions, or who lend our support to them, must be part of the change within them, always encouraging them to become the best they can be, responsible and ethical. These institutions are reflections of ourselves. We ought to be proud of them, not ashamed of them.

Again, each of us has an important role to play in bringing about real transformation.

HEALTH CARE

In America, our current health care system is completely immoral and a disgrace to our nation. By putting profits over people, the system is causing the unnecessary suffering and deaths of untold millions.

> *"My name is Wendell Potter, and for 20 years, I worked as a senior executive at health insurance companies, and I saw how they confuse their customers and dump the sick — all so they can satisfy their Wall Street investors."* ~ Wendell Potter, testimony before a Senate panel investigating the health care industry, 2009

Let me say it again: health care is a basic human right, not a privilege to be enjoyed by a wealthy few.

Every human being on this Earth needs and deserves access to adequate and compassionate care. That ought to be our goal. Then we need to figure out how to achieve it.

What can you do?

- Join and support the people and organizations that are fighting for universal health care.
- Let your representatives, national, state and local, know loud and clear that you demand quality, affordable health care for all.
- If you are a part of the health care industry, do your part to change it and make it more compassionate.
- Take responsibility for your own personal health. Exercise regularly and choose a healthy diet. The healthier you are, the less you will need to utilize health care services.
- Support free clinics to provide health care for those who can't afford it.
- Support humanitarian organizations that provide health care services for those in need all over the world.

Finally, lest anyone misinterpret what I'm saying here, the problem is with our system, not with most of the individuals who are participating in the system. There are, of course, many wonderful, caring doctors, nurses and other health care providers who are genuinely committed to helping their patients. They are among the 4's and 5's who do heroic service every day. They recognize that the system is broken and desperately needs fixing. They will be instrumental in providing the guidance and leadership that will finally implement a reformed system of health care that will live up to its moral imperative to take care of all of our citizens.

There is absolutely no reason that the U.S. health care system can't be among the most advanced, the most affordable, the most comprehensive, and the most ethical in the entire world.

THE MILITARY-INDUSTRIAL COMPLEX

"Every gun that is made, every warship launched, every rocket fired signifies, in the final sense, a theft from those who hunger and are not fed, those who are cold and are not clothed. This world in arms is not spending money alone. It is spending the sweat of its laborers, the genius of its scientists, the hopes of its children." ~ Dwight D. Eisenhower[88]

The extraordinary power and influence of the military-industrial complex ought to be of grave concern to us all. Their most destructive weapon is not a ship, a plane, or a bomb. Their most destructive weapon is fear. Fear gives them their power. As long as they can keep us fearful, they can continue to go on conducting business as usual. Millions of people, innocent people, will continue to die.

"A nation that continues year after year to spend more money on military defense than on programs of social uplift is approaching spiritual doom." ~ Rev. Dr. Martin Luther King, Jr.[89]

Military defense is one thing. Military offense is another. The latter is not acceptable from civilized nations in a civilized world. The Bush Doctrine,[90] holding that the U.S. can make war on foreign regimes merely for a *perceived* threat to U.S. interests, is simply immoral. Talk about a violation of the One Idea! It's an Anti-Golden Rule: Bomb others before they can bomb you!

We all recognize the need for *adequate* military defense. That's not the issue; that's sensible in a world fraught with distress. But greed has a way of getting out of control. Greed knows no limits. Those entrenched in the military-industrial complex have a financial incentive to develop unnecessary military programs and create unnecessary wars just to line their pockets.

Do you want to talk about evil? What do you call it when people make money off the killing of other human beings, especially completely innocent human beings – women, children, the elderly, the sick, the poor? Can anyone stoop lower than that? You tell me.

I want to make it clear, however, that I mean no disrespect for the honorable individuals who serve in the military. I come from a long line of ancestors who have risked their lives to proudly serve their country in times of war. The vast majority of our service men and women serve unselfishly and with distinction. Many are among our very finest citizens. They are not the problem.

Again, the problem is systemic. The system, driven by greed, too often risks the lives of our military men and women foolishly and unnecessarily. Too many people have been killed and maimed, too many families have been destroyed, in conflicts that could have been avoided, conflicts that are perpetrated more for the economic or political gain of a powerful elite, than for any legitimate, worthwhile national interests.

What can you do?

- Vote for people with both wisdom and compassion to lead us. We need more peacemakers and fewer warmongers.
- Speak out against war and those who profit from it.
- Object to the exorbitant use of tax dollars to fund wasteful military spending.
- Support diplomatic solutions to foreign policy issues.
- Support veterans and veterans' issues.
- Be an advocate for peace.
- Support organized groups that are working for peace around the world.
- Beware of overbearing nationalism. We need to think globally as world citizens, build trust and honor our interconnection.
- Insist on justice for military war crimes.
- Insist the U.S. abide by the Geneva Conventions.[91] Torture is not only barbaric and disgraceful, it doesn't work.

BUCKET #7: THE BANKS, WALL STREET, AND OTHER FINANCIAL INSTITUTIONS

Many would contend that the real apex predators out there – the 6's and 7's with the most power, influence and control that are causing so much trouble and suffering – are the Big Banks, Wall Street and other financial institutions. Their business is money. It seems safe to say that most people who make their living through these financial organizations are driven by a fair amount of greed. Have they become so engrossed in their dollars and cents, amassing their profits day by day, that they have lost sight of their humanity? Have they forgotten what it truly means to be human and part of the Earth?

If you are one of these people, we might wonder what kind of person you really are and ask you, as a matter of conscience, to dig deep into the ethical questions surrounding your business. Can you unequivocally say you are part of making this world a better place? Does your business truly help people without hurting others?

This is a call to conscience. Are you listening?

It may be that we need a complete overhaul of our economic system. It seems very apparent that it will have to evolve along more humanitarian lines if our civilization is to survive. There are many out there who have the expertise and some sound, practical ideas that can move us forward as a global community. At all times, in this as in everything else, we must keep the One Idea in mind. Compassion will save us; greed and exploitation will kill us.

A GENERAL RULE

"Compassion is the basis of all morality." ~ Arthur Schopenhauer, philosopher (1788-1860)

It is very important that all of us stand up for what is right. What is right is based on the common good, compassion for all – the One Idea. All of us are in the bucket brigade that must put out the flames.

We need to reconnect with one another in our local communities and discuss the relevant issues that plague us. Organized groups with specific targets of interest and concern can be much more effective than individuals working alone.

I suggest that, as a general rule, we should praise individuals and corporations/institutions when they do the right thing and hold them accountable when they do the wrong thing. We do the same thing when we raise our children, don't we?

Public condemnation goes a long way in establishing what is and what is not acceptable in a society. The public good will prevail if the public demands it.

So, what are you waiting for?

"You can't cross the sea merely by standing and staring at the water." ~ Rabindranath Tagore, poet

WHO ME?

Yes, that's right, I'm talking to you! Turn off the TV, get your butt off the couch and DO something. I have a bucket right here that will come in handy!

All of us are part of the problem, but all of us together can also be the solution. In fact, the truth is, unless we come together, at least the majority of us, and really begin to change the world for the better, we will ultimately destroy ourselves.

"When the people lead, the leaders will follow." ~ Margaret Mead

We The People must lead the way. When we make our voices heard in numbers that are overwhelming, our leaders will have no choice but to follow. Our institutions themselves will fundamentally change.

"Truth will ultimately prevail where there is pains taken to bring it to light." ~ George Washington[92]

Let us never forget that we have the power to create whatever world we want. We collectively created the mess that we see before us. We can also create a world that works. Many good people have already shown us the way.

In the next chapter, we will discuss how you, too, can join the ranks of the greatest and most admirable human beings of all time. You know who they are – many of them are quoted in this book. They always inspire us, by their words and their deeds, to strive for positive change. You, too, can become one of the 4's or the 5's, the real heroes who will put out the fire and set this world aright.

CHAPTER SIX

The Real Heroes

CHAPTER SIX

The Real Heroes

"Everybody thinks of changing humanity, and nobody thinks of changing himself." ~ Leo Tolstoy[93]

Change begins with each of us as individuals. We don't have the power to change anyone else. Not really. We can influence people, yes, but... we only have the power to change ourselves. So why don't we become the best that we can be? That is the real challenge, isn't it?

Dare to find your own truth, despite what others say, then have the courage to live it. Allow your personal integrity to guide you.

"I resolve to speak ill of no man whatever... and upon proper occasions speak all the good I know of every body." ~ Benjamin Franklin [94]

"When angry, count ten before you speak; if very angry, an hundred." ~ Thomas Jefferson [95]

Let's make sure our words and actions are contributing to the health and well-being of us all. Let's set a standard for others to look up to, especially our children. Ours is a grave responsibility and we need to take it very seriously.

Most importantly, we need to get involved. We need to take action. This will be very frustrating at times, for it may seem that no one is paying any attention. It may seem as if no one really cares. We must always remember, however, that while we can never know how we impact so many others, we certainly do. That's part of what interconnectedness is all about.

That's a very comforting thought, isn't it? Everything we do matters.

"Never doubt that a small group of thoughtful, committed citizens can change the world. Indeed, it is the only thing that ever has." ~ Margaret Mead

The numbers of 4's and 5's out there, those who will change and save the world, is growing. You may already be one of them, or perhaps you're working on being the change. After all, at one time or another we have all been 1's, 2's, or 3's, maybe even 6's or 7's when we are at our mean-spirited worst. We might also vary in our approach from one issue to another. For example, a person may be a 4 when it comes to littering, picking up after others and helping to keep the environment clean, while at the same time being a 1 when it comes to climate change, denying that there is even a problem.

We must always remember that people are complex, capable of both good and bad. Nothing in this world is black or white. We are always dealing with many different shades of gray. No one should be demonized.

In this chapter, we're going to take a closer look at ourselves – our values and behaviors. If we are contributing to the flames that are engulfing us, we need to become aware and make a sincere effort to change ourselves.

THE REAL HERO IS YOU

At this point in this book, you understand the One Idea, that we are all One, interconnected. You understand how many of our institutions, the systems that we have created, have been corrupted by greed and selfishness. You understand that the house is burning; the world is on fire. You understand that it's your world. It's your house that is on fire. Your loved ones are trapped inside, your children and your grandchildren and all of our descendants in times to come.

Future generations have no power to avert the disaster that awaits them. By the time they are born, it will be too late. Only we can save them.

Everything we do or don't do today will have an impact on the future.

"You cannot escape the responsibility of tomorrow by evading it today." ~ Abraham Lincoln

The success or failure of our entire civilization is dependent upon you as well as every other human being on the planet. We all bear equal responsibility here. Collectively we create the future for good or for ill. You cannot escape your collective responsibility any more than you can escape your individual responsibility.

Moreover, you know in the goodness of your heart what is required. You understand the need for love and compassion. "Do unto others as you would have them do unto you." You can't escape the truth of the Golden Rule.

So now it's up to you. You have a bucket in your hand. What are you going to do with it? You can't just walk away, can you? You wouldn't do that to your children and grandchildren.

"Those who have the privilege to know, have the duty to act." ~ Albert Einstein

With knowledge comes responsibility. Now that you understand that the house is on fire, you cannot be a 1, 2 or 3, ignoring what's happening or pretending that somehow the problems will magically disappear without your having to lift a finger. That's not acceptable. You don't have the luxury of being able to ignore the truth of what is happening here. There are too many people depending on you. You have to choose. It's a simple choice really. It's the difference between right and wrong.

There's plenty we can all do to douse the flames. Each one of us. The question is not so much what CAN we do, the question is what WILL we do?

You see this is all about *will*. Do we have the will, both individually and collectively as a species, to do the right thing?

Think of all those heroes you've idolized over the years in movies and books. Why were they deserving of your admiration? They were people of indomitable will who never gave in to the forces that opposed them.

The people who change the world never lose hope no matter how bleak the outcome might appear to be.

Well, guess what? Take a look in the mirror. You're the hero of this real-life action thriller! This is humanity's last stand on planet Earth. Take pride in being one of the fighters for truth and justice. Take pride in being the culmination of the hopes and dreams of all of your ancestors from the beginning of time. Take pride in being a 4 or a 5! There may seem to be only a few now, but more people are awakening every day. More help is on the way!

> *"There's some good in this world, Mr. Frodo. And it's worth fighting for."* ~ Sam Gamgee[96]

On their epic journey in J.R.R. Tolkien's *The Lord of the Rings*, Frodo Baggins and Samwise Gamgee had a specific goal in mind. They knew where they had to go and what they had to do to save the world: they had to cast the ring of power into the fires of Mt. Doom.

Our path to our own salvation is not so simple or clear cut. This isn't fantasy. This is real life. We're going to have to identify the problem areas that need our attention and make significant changes in the way we think and in the way we live our lives.

The truth about where we need to be, the roadmap that will show us the way is very clear: it's the One Idea. We must care about one another, work together and focus on what is best for all. If we do so, step by small step, we will change – and save – the world. Our grandchildren will inherit a sustainable world, not a depleted and devastated one.

> *"The journey of a thousand miles begins with one step."* ~ Lao Tsu[97]

The first step is to understand what's happening. The ring of power we have to destroy is our own selfishness and greed. Mt. Doom is that dark, forbidding place within our own hearts. A change of heart will require a change in values.

THREE FUNDAMENTAL CHANGES IN OUR VALUE SYSTEM

"We as a nation must undergo a radical revolution of values. We must rapidly begin the shift from a 'thing oriented' society to a 'person oriented' society. When machines and computers, profit motives and property rights are considered more important than people, the giant triplets of racism, materialism and militarism are incapable of being conquered." ~ Rev. Dr. Martin Luther King, Jr.[98]

There are three fundamental changes we each need to make in our value system in order to move us to where we need to be.

1. **We must value one another and planet Earth over the accumulation of money, material goods and power.**
   This will require that we make decisions based on the wisdom of long-term considerations for the greater good, rather than short-term financial gain for the few.
2. **We must value truth.**
   We must demand honesty and integrity from our leaders, the media, our businesses and our institutions and hold them accountable when they fail.
3. **We must value generosity.**
   We must rise above our arrogance and our selfish egos to become truly caring people who gladly give of themselves to help others.

This is really all about love again, isn't it? We must love one another as ourselves and overcome our petty, ego-driven desires. Compassion and empathy will be critical to our spiritual transformation.

The cynics, of course, will say that such a global spiritual transformation is impossible. They're wrong. Anything is possible. If you don't believe me, study some quantum physics!

On a very personal level, what you focus on, what you observe becomes your reality, your own personal truth. Unfortunately, many of us make the mistake of thinking that our personal truths are absolute truths, applicable to all. To be honest with yourself and others, you must always acknowledge the truth may be other than what you perceive it to be.

Here again we're talking about open-mindedness.

What we really need is a majority of the people on the planet to make the shift to compassionate consciousness. In fact, I think the majority of people on the planet already agree with these values and would be willing to commit to them wholeheartedly – IF they understood the truth about what's happening, the urgency of the situation, and how to go about effecting change.

"So then, putting away falsehood, let all of us speak the truth to our neighbors, for we are members of one another." ~ Ephesians 4:25

There's that One Idea again! The reality is that too many people on the planet are now living in darkness. They don't even understand what's happening. Many have been deceived by the duplicitous propaganda of the 6's and 7's who don't have their best interests at heart.

THE REALITY OF OUR DIFFERENT WORLDS

Speaking of reality, let's try a short exercise here. We are going to explore three different worlds or levels of reality that exist simultaneously and may or may not require our attention, depending on our needs at any given point in time.

- The Internal World
- The Immediate External World
- The Greater External World

THE INTERNAL WORLD

First, find a nice private, quiet place and close your eyes. Go within. Relax. Get really comfortable inside yourself. This is the safest place you will ever be. This is your internal world. This is your reality. It includes your thoughts and beliefs, your feelings, your memories, and all your life experience.

Your internal world is completely unique from anyone else's. Remember that. Remember that we are all very different and perceive the world in different ways depending upon our own experiences. In this sense, we all have very different perceptions of what we call "reality." If we want to be compassionate and forgiving, we must understand that others see and experience the world differently. We have no idea, really, who they are and what they have experienced in their lives. We should refrain from judging anyone too harshly.

"Judge not, lest ye be judged." ~ Matthew 7:1-5

In this internal world, no one else is here physically except you. All of your troubles are outside yourself. They can't bother you here unless you allow them into your thoughts. It's just you here. You can control what thoughts you entertain and what you dismiss. Choose to be at peace with yourself and enjoy the experience. Drop all those negative thoughts and just concentrate on your breath. The breath of life. Feel the miracle of being alive. You are just like all of your ancestors; you breathe the same air. How good to be alive! All of your descendants in times to come, will take this breath too, just like you. It is a breath we all share. We are all connected. This is the place of true peace. We all have access to it almost any time we choose.

Wouldn't it be wonderful if we could take this feeling of peace and give it to the whole world?

"Blessed are the peacemakers..." ~ Matthew 5:9

A friend of mine once remarked, "It's hard to imagine world peace." Peace is as easy to imagine as conflict, violence, or war. Live what you believe. If you believe in peace, live it. Make peace with those in your own life with whom you have issues.

When there is peace in the world you create within you and around you, you will find happiness, despite the greater conflicts that happen in the larger world outside of your direct influence and control.

"If we have no peace, it is because we have forgotten that we belong to each other." ~ Mother Teresa[99]

Closing our eyes and getting in touch with ourselves also puts us in touch with the entire Universe. It is a place of prayer and meditation. Here we can reconnect with the deepest spiritual truths.

I liken this internal world, this level of consciousness, to the quantum level of the Universe. It is an energy field from which the physical realities of our lives emerge. Scientists tell us that the Big Bang emerged from an infinitesimal singularity condition without time or space.[100] In effect, matter emerged out of "nothingness." The same happens with our own consciousness. The physical, material things that we create in our lives begin as ideas or dreams. This book, for example, came out of the cosmic soup of my consciousness, which is, of course, connected to the greater collective consciousness of all.

This interior world is the domain of creativity. Artists know this place very well. It is an amazing place to be, yet in our modern fast-moving lifestyles, few of us take the time to visit it and rejuvenate our spirits. So many nowadays seem unable to even disconnect from a cell phone or a computer or a television screen.

"Your vision will become clear only when you can look into your own heart. Who looks outside dreams; who looks inside awakens." ~ Carl Jung

All of us need to take time with ourselves, to quietly reflect on who we are, and explore our connection to the infinite. For some this means getting in touch with God. Whatever your spiritual beliefs, your quiet time in reflection is an important part of living a healthy and satisfying life.

Now that you have found your inner peace, the quiet place inside yourself that is connected to the whole, without judgment or fear, let's open our eyes and engage the immediate external world.

"Out beyond ideas of wrongdoing and rightdoing, there is a field. I'll meet you there." ~ Rumi

Techno-Man

I'm plugged in. wigged out. logged on.
To the wall.
Brain-wired
Through windows of intercyber space
Tele-marketed on airwaves of
High-tech no resolution
Toastered in a micro-waved oven
Ears popped corn-wise
My electric eyes spin in sockets
Juiced like a jingled julep
Sucked through the jargon
Of video laser loserlips
Played for a lackey
By big no-name hucksters who think
I have no will of my own.
But if I pull the plug
Now
Will self and soul re-boot
Or just be
(Deleted).

THE IMMEDIATE EXTERNAL WORLD

Look around you. This is your immediate external world. What do you see? As I sit in my office typing this at my desk, I see a lot of things in the room: my computer, my bookcase, my files, a closet, etc. My wife is at her computer nearby. We have a wonderful relationship. There is no conflict or distress here. This is my reality at this point in time. In this immediate external reality, I am completely at home. There is peace in this little world. There is no conflict here, only love.

Now let me broaden this little world a bit. I look out the window, I see the quaint gray house across the street and rain falling on wet grass.

There are no people as far as I can see. No cars on the road... I hear a train whistle in the distance. What a beautiful scene. Very serene. My entire visible world at this point in time is at peace. Any conflicts I place into this world, created by negative thoughts in my head, do not exist in this physical reality, they are creations of my mind. But I'm not going to entertain any negative thoughts. I'm choosing to stay with the peaceful immediate external world. I am going to enjoy this moment.

We all make these choices all the time. Are we addicted to or obsessed with the negatives in our lives? Do we find our thoughts constantly returning to our problems? Are we in love with the drama of conflict? Do we, in fact, enjoy the pain?

We enter any number of little external worlds on a daily basis: our living room, the dining room, the interior of our car, our place of work, the grocery store, the restaurant, the movie theater, church, etc. Most of the time for most of us, there aren't any horrible conflicts in these places; sure there might be occasional disturbances now and then as people move through various levels of anger and frustration, but most of the time there is peace. People are politely going about their day.

Believe it or not, most of us in our daily lives, live in states of virtual peace. When others come into our little worlds, they carry their own needs and desires and, if we allow it, there is the potential for conflict. Do we avert it? confront it? provoke it? At every moment, we make choices. When we become aware of a choice in the making, then we can choose a positive, rather than a negative energy. We might choose to be polite and attentive, for example, rather than to be sneering and dismissive when conversing with a colleague on an issue of concern.

The Honorable Intention

I keep a word inside my head
At all times—
Respect.

Only with such a word
Can honor be
Upheld.

Little choices every day shape who we are; they shape our relationships with others, our relationships with the world, and our relationships with the Universe. Our physical, mental and emotional health are largely dependent upon the health of these relationships. In many instances, we create the conflicts ourselves and often these conflicts only exist in our own minds.

"Some of the worst things in my life never happened."

~ Mark Twain

We cannot get inside someone else's skin and truly understand what they think or feel, so we guess. Usually, we make guesses based on our own insecurities and inadequate perceptions. Psychologists call this projection. Webster's defines projection as "the tendency to ascribe to another person feelings, thoughts, or attitudes present in oneself, or to regard external reality as embodying such feelings, thoughts, etc., in some way." [101]

When we project our own thoughts, feelings and attitudes onto others, we are not dealing with reality. We are dealing with our own perception of reality, which may be inaccurate.

As we become more aware of the One Idea and how it can impact our everyday lives, we take a better, more accurate look at the world around us, whatever little world we're in.

Ask yourself, who besides myself inhabits this world at present? Am I at peace with these people? Are there any issues with our relationships? Any negative feelings, conflicts or disturbances? If so, we should probably address them, because they usually do not go away of their own accord. But let's address them wisely – always keeping the One Idea in mind with compassion in our hearts.

Nowadays, people are becoming much more crass, cruel and abusive in their language with others. The language we choose is very important. If we are mindful, we will be respectful.

"Whatever words we utter should be chosen with care for people will hear them and be influenced by them for good or ill."

~ Bukkyo Dendo Kyokai, *The Teaching of Buddha* [102]

It is very important to listen to what the other person is saying and try to understand where he/she is really coming from. Sometimes, unfortunately, there will be a divide that cannot be bridged. It's no use trying to reasonably argue with unreasonable people. Better to spend your time in more productive pursuits. At the same time, beware of those who try to convince you through reason to be unreasonable.

"...re-examine all you have been told at school or church or in any book, dismiss whatever insults your own soul..." ~ Walt Whitman[103]

Sometimes people will insist on being confrontational and aggressive, in which case you have a choice to make. You can be equally combative and escalate the hostility, or you can choose not to allow the person to get to you. This requires conscious effort and can be difficult to learn at first, but as you practice, it will become easier. Often, it will defuse the situation completely and lead to a satisfactory resolution. This is the wisdom inherent in "If someone strikes you on the right cheek, turn to him the other one also."[104] We don't have to demean ourselves by engaging in abusive, immature behavior or succumbing to the spiritual illness of others.

Those who create peace in their immediate external worlds do all of us a favor. The positive energy they generate is a pleasure to be around.

We can all feel the love when we walk into a healthy environment. We feel welcome and appreciated just for being who we are. Any place of business knows this to be true. You want your customers to feel special. Alienate your customers and they'll walk out the door and never come back!

"Our company was founded 110 years ago on The Golden Rule, which is about treating people fair and square, just like you would like to be treated yourself." ~ Ron Johnson, CEO, jcpenney[105]

Imagine how much healthier our society would be if we could all create kind and compassionate work places, in which we address conflicts wisely and work toward respectful resolutions. This shouldn't be very hard to do. It's just basic human decency.

Everyone wants a friendly, calm, cooperative work environment. If our relationships with our co-workers are amiable and respectful, even the most odious of jobs can be done with equanimity.

The hardest "little world" to deal with, however, is the home – our relationships with our immediate families and significant others. These relationships, for all of us, represent the greatest personal challenges of our lives.

Think about it. What's the most difficult thing to do in life? Is it to climb Mt. Everest or is it to truly love others with unconditional love? Love is not easy. It takes time and effort and sincere dedication. But it is worth it, every step of the way.

> *"For one human being to love another: that is perhaps the most difficult of all our tasks, the ultimate, the last test and proof, the work for which all other work is but preparation."*
> ~ Rainer Maria Rilke[106]

Just as in our dealings with others at work, we need to be kind, courteous, and respectful with each member of our family. We really need to work on building healthy, loving relationships. This will require time and honest communication. Family counseling may also be very helpful.

Like climbing Mt. Everest the journey to all-encompassing love will be incredibly difficult, often painful, but if in the end as you lie on your deathbed you can say, "I love everyone and everything with all my heart," then you will have reached the summit and accomplished what very few people truly accomplish: a life filled with love and a sense of complete fulfillment and satisfaction. May we all reach that summit, plant our flags and say "I was here" before we die.

THE GREATER EXTERNAL WORLD

When we open a newspaper or magazine, turn on the TV, connect to the Internet, or attend a public event, we are permitting the greater external world to come into our immediate external world. Sometimes it seems more like an invasion than an invitation. We are exposing ourselves to all the negativity that the greater world entails. We are opening ourselves up to what is going on in the wide, wide world. Much of it is unpleasant. There are the larger travesties like murder and mayhem and then there are the subtler little murders that happen on a large scale every day by people treating one another with contempt or derision in one way or another. There is lack of opportunity, joblessness and hopelessness. There are wars, poverty, hunger, desperation, and despair. There are natural disasters and terrible diseases.

The One Idea compels us to be sensitive to the suffering of others and to do what we can to alleviate it. All the great religions and all the great humanitarians agree on this point.

> *"What does love look like? It has the hands to help others. It has the feet to hasten to the poor and needy. It has eyes to see misery and want. It has the ears to hear the sighs and sorrows of men. That is what love looks like."* ~ Saint Augustine (354-430 CE)

It is not easy to do – to devote oneself to helping others. Many of the 4's and 5's are involved in such work on a daily basis. It requires strength and courage, as well as love and patience, to continually engage the suffering in the greater world in a positive, healthy manner. The work can be very draining (though it can also be incredibly rewarding). Some people simply aren't up to the task. Some of the 3's, for example, might become so disturbed by the harsh truths in the world, that they can't even bear to think about them. They aren't emotionally equipped to deal with them in any way.

Still, we all need to do what we can. We cannot, in good conscience, turn our backs on the suffering of others.

At the same time, we all need to pay attention to our personal health and retreat periodically, as needed, to our smaller worlds for rejuvenation. That's why we all need vacations – opportunities to get away from the daily grind and choose more positive experiences. We need to spend quality time with ourselves and others.

It's always important to remember that, for most of us most of the time, the greater external world with all its difficulties is really outside ourselves. Most of what we know of it comes second-hand – from others. We are not in direct physical contact with it. It's not a part of our internal world unless we allow it to come in. When it begins to overwhelm us, we can disconnect from it by focusing elsewhere. At such times, it can be very helpful to reconnect with the infinite.

THE UNIVERSE AROUND US

Going within ourselves can connect us to the infinite. Gazing at the sky, the mountains, or the ocean can do the same thing. There is peace to be found in detaching ourselves from the everyday cacophony of our overpopulated Earth and letting our minds wander into the vastness of the greater natural world. We begin to see the Big Picture. I find the clear night sky to be particularly healing – the moon, the stars, the tranquil darkness twinkling with light.

When we get in touch with the immensity of the Universe, we feel the endless possibility of what this miracle life is all about. We are but a tiny part, but we are an important part. Without each of us, the Universe is incomplete. With us, the Universe fulfills itself. Anything is possible. We are only limited by our imaginations.

PEACE WITHIN AND WITHOUT

Now that we've taken a look at these three different worlds or levels of reality – The Internal World, The Immediate External World, and The Greater External World – we can begin to assess our own understanding of the One Idea. How can we make peace with ourselves and the world around us?

Peace and love are not idealistic improbabilities; they are very definite possibilities within the scope of each and every individual relationship.

In some ways we have become addicted to the argumentative, the confrontational, the combative. Part of this is cultural and part of it may be biological, but we need to understand that peace and love cannot become prevalent around the world until the majority of people relinquish the need to make war with themselves and others.

Those who mock and denigrate peace, love, and compassion – and there are many such people out there – have been wounded in some way. Like children, they are acting out their anger, their frustration, and their pain. On some level, they derive enjoyment out of being cruel. It is a way of exacting revenge for the wrongs they have suffered. We should not take such behavior personally. It is a symptom of spiritual illness.

They are in denial of the One Idea. They live in the illusion that people are separate.

"At this time in history, we are to take nothing personally. Least of all, ourselves! For the moment we do, our spiritual growth and journey comes to an end. The time of the Lone Wolf is over!"
~ Thomas Banyacya Sr., Elder of the Hopi Nation

As we begin to live the One Idea, always focusing on a commitment to being kind, compassionate and forgiving, we will find our relationships becoming healthier. As each of us makes positive changes to our immediate external worlds, so too will the greater external world change around us.

Peace is not an unachievable dream. It is certainly achievable on a personal level. All of us have the power to find and create peace within ourselves. This is our first challenge. Then, we can extend love and peace outward to include others.

Real World

I seem to be slipping from the real world
the world of making money and paying bills

I've grown uncomfortable with the ritual
of going to and fro

unmindful of the journey
the play of grasses in the wind

I seem to want the solitude
the earth upon my hands

the stillness of the water
the quiet of the night

I seem to be maturing
a fruit ripening on the vine.

As we commit to peace in our own lives, our own little worlds, encompassing everyone we know personally, then we will find the way of peace spreading like a great healing light all over the world.

FORGIVENESS

"...we are saved by the final form of love, which is forgiveness."
~ Reinhold Niebuhr[107]

Forgiveness is key to personal transformation. We all have done some pretty hurtful things in our time. We are, after all, flawed human beings. We need to forgive those who have harmed us and ask forgiveness for those we have wronged. And finally, we must forgive ourselves.

The road to genuine forgiveness is a tough one, but we all need to make the journey. It takes real determination to forgive someone for a deep physical or spiritual offense, but you will never be truly free until you do. You may want to seek the help of healing professionals.

Forgiveness is so important that it should be a priority. Your success will dramatically transform your immediate external world, the world of your family, friends and acquaintances. As you release the anger and the bitterness, you will feel differently about everything and others will feel differently about you. Love is infectious.

Forgiveness

requires putting aside the ego to acknowledge

the inter-connection of

one human being to another.

In forgiveness, we acknowledge the flaws in us all. We all have our share of problems and challenges. There is no such thing as a perfect human being.

"There is a crack in everything. That's how the light gets in." ~ Leonard Cohen[108]

Even as we live the One Idea and the Golden Rule, we still won't be perfect. We will still make mistakes. That's what it is to be human. But with forgiveness in our hearts, we will find ourselves becoming a more positive and healing presence in the world.

PARENTING

"Life affords no greater responsibility, no greater privilege, than the raising of the next generation." ~ C. Everett Koop, Former U.S. Surgeon General[109]

As we focus on the One Idea and seek to be a positive force for good, we recognize how vitally important our relationships are. There is probably no more important job than the loving parenting of our children.

Society pays a huge price for inadequate and abusive parenting. Children who are not properly loved and cared for become physically and mentally ill. Severe physical or emotional abuse or neglect can destroy a child's entire life.

"What a child doesn't receive he can seldom later give."
~ P.D. James, author[110]

Many parents are wounded themselves, having been poorly raised by parents who were wounded as children. So you see, the wounds are handed down from generation to generation. Wounded people take out their anger and frustration on others. The whole world is thereby made sick.

Quite frankly, this is where we find ourselves right now – in a very sick world that ignores the power of love. We now know a lot about healthy, loving parenting techniques. Why don't we teach some basic parental skills as part of a good high school education? Isn't that just common sense?

Why is it that, in so many ways, we have lost our common sense?

Too many of us have bought into the idea that our jobs, our careers, our hobbies, are more important, more worthy of our time, than our families. Imagine how much better our world would be if we gave our families the attention they deserve, spending plenty of quality time communicating and enjoying one another's company. How much happier would we all be?

"If you treat your children like they are the most interesting people you know, they probably will be." ~ Rosalie Sorrels, musician[111]

Healthy families know how to laugh, even when times get rough. In fact, one of the most important things you can teach your kids is to have a sense of humor in the face of life's difficulties.

Unfortunately, for most of us, our jobs consume far more time and energy than we are ever able to devote to our families. We spend eight to twelve hours or more at our jobs, come home exhausted, plop ourselves down in front of a TV and zone out. This is the world we have collectively created for ourselves. We have been conditioned to value work and the making of money over the far more important need to create happy, healthy relationships with those we dearly love.

If

when you look into your child's eyes
you do not see the future

then

you have not understood
the meaning

of your place in the Universe.

Jobs will pass away and really mean very little in the great scheme of things, but relationships transcend time. The people you love in your life are with you always, whether or not they still walk on this Earth.

When you die, you will continue to live on in the hearts of those who love you. This is what life is all about.

EDUCATION

> *"The illiterate of the 21st century will not be those who cannot read and write, but those who cannot learn, unlearn, and relearn."* ~ Alvin Toffler

Education is essential to putting out the flames that are destroying our house. The 4's and 5's know they must be part of a continual, ongoing effort to educate themselves and the rest of the world. All of us need to understand, as best we can, the difficulties that face us so that we can wisely take appropriate action.

Information and its relevance changes over time. Some things once thought to be true may be proven false later, so it is important to stay on top of new developments.

> *"Wisdom lies only in truth."* ~ Johann Wolfgang von Goethe[112]

We should always seek the truth. With so much propaganda and misinformation out there, the truth can be very difficult, if not impossible, to find. It is shocking that even children's textbooks are being altered to promote specific political, religious and ideological agendas.[113]

> *"Facts are stubborn things; and whatever may be our wishes, our inclinations, or the dictates of our passions, they cannot alter the state of facts and evidence."* ~ John Adams[114]

We need to seek out factual, non-biased sources. We need to listen to the wisest among us who have all of our best interests at heart.

Most importantly, we need to support the education of our children. Certainly, public schools have a lot of problems and in some respects are failing. I know. In my career, I've taught in dozens of them. I've seen the best and the worst. I must say, however, that there are far more good schools than poor schools.

But when our schools fail, we all bear some responsibility. Every child has a right to a quality education. In every community, we must ensure that this is so. You can't keep cutting the funding to our schools and expect them to get better. They will only get worse. Again, it's a matter of priorities.

As a society, we need to value education far more than we do. Education should be a top priority. The success of our economy depends on having a highly educated, highly skilled workforce. We won't be able to compete in a global economy when our students are failing in key subjects like math, science, reading, and writing. No student should be permitted to graduate without demonstrating competence in all of these areas.

Everything is interconnected, remember? As our educational system declines, so does our economy and our quality of life.

It is essential that we spend the necessary dollars to make our system among the best in the world.[115] This would include paying our teachers a decent salary.[116] Teaching is one of the noblest of professions and should be respected as such, yet in the U.S. we pay our teachers miserably, compared to many other less meaningful and less stressful occupations. Teachers work very hard. Their jobs are incredibly difficult and, at the same time, extremely important. They are instrumental to the success or failure of our children and the future of our nation.

"The only thing more expensive than education is ignorance."
~ Benjamin Franklin

Funding cuts do serious damage. As jobs are lost and teachers get laid off, class sizes are increased to the point where they become almost unmanageable. Most teachers would agree that classes larger than 25 students are counterproductive and will impede the learning process of every student in the class. Teachers need to be able to spend quality time with each of their students.

Music, art, theatre, and physical education are often the first subjects to feel the budget axe. When these programs are cut, our children's mental and emotional well being, as well as their education, suffers.

"The object of the educational system, taken as a whole, is not to produce hands for industry or to teach the young how to make a living. It is to produce responsible citizens." ~ Robert Maynard Hutchins, educational philosopher[117]

Too many Americans haven't got a clue what being a responsible citizen is all about. They don't even know who their representatives are or how the government works. It truly is appalling. As I said previously, our schools ought to provide comprehensive courses in government, civics, and American history.

"Knowledge will forever govern ignorance; and a people who mean to be their own governors must arm themselves with the power which knowledge gives." ~ James Madison[118]

We all pay a steep price for the ignorance and utter lack of intellectual curiosity that pervades American culture. If we are going to have any long-term success in putting out the flames we have to improve our educational system. Here are some more ideas worthy of consideration.

- Teach critical thinking skills. This is so important in these modern times when it is so difficult to distinguish between fact and fiction.
- Provide access to computers and other technology that will help children to succeed.
- Provide environmental education. Give students opportunities to reconnect with nature.
- Repair or replace deteriorating school buildings. We need to provide clean, safe, comfortable learning environments for all.
- Provide nutritious meals for students. Child obesity is a big problem in this country. Junk food should not be on the menu.
- Let educators be educators. Too often politicians, bureaucrats and administrative types who are not trained or qualified as educators are making the decisions that affect our children's education. They are even designing the overall programs of instruction. Let's allow our educators to do their jobs and create the programs that will best serve students.

A lot of these issues are beyond our individual control. We need the people in power to become 4's and 5's and implement strategies for productive change. But what can you do as an ordinary citizen? Do you support your public schools and your local libraries? Do you volunteer? Do you vote for bond measures that will improve education? Have you ever served on a school board?

Most importantly, if you have children of your own, do you take an active role in your children's education, getting to know their teachers, helping with their homework, communicating with them frequently to assess how they are doing? Communication is very important. Many kids are being bullied at school and their parents don't even know about it. Bullying is a big problem. This should not be surprising given all the irresponsible, cruel bullying behavior we see all the time in the adult world, particularly in our media and in our politics. Our children are mimicking what they see. Innocent lives are being senselessly lost because of it.

Going to school ought to be an enjoyable experience for everyone. Children should not dread going to school. Learning should be fun. The best teachers are very creative in the ways they engage their students. Schools ought to foster and support innovative teaching methods.

Our schools and our teachers need to inspire children to love learning so that they will continue to educate themselves long after they get out of school. If schools fail in this regard, they are failing in their most important mission.

The Real Heroes will put a strong emphasis on education as we move forward. They know we need to get our priorities straight.

DEMOCRACY – ALL ARE CREATED EQUAL

The healthy world we seek will be based on equality. Equality of all people. No one should be oppressed.

"We hold these truths to be self-evident that all men are created equal..." ~ Declaration of Independence, 1776

Equality is an idea that our Founding Fathers enshrined in American democracy, though at the time the idea really only encompassed free males who owned property. As we have become more enlightened, as our hearts have opened, we realize that all people should be equal in all respects and have the same rights to "life, liberty, and the pursuit of happiness."

Laws in a democracy should ensure that this is so.

Democracy, in theory, gives everyone a voice. Freedom of speech is very important. We need a free and open exchange of ideas. It is particularly important to preserve a free and open Internet, which has been so instrumental to giving voice to the aspirations of ordinary people around the world. We must guard against the continuing efforts of corporate and government entities trying to undermine our Internet freedoms in their pursuit of profits and power.

Democracy is a very positive development in the history of the human race and will help us to achieve the sustainable world that we envision. Authoritarianism, on the other hand, is a violation of the One Idea and is naturally abhorrent to all freedom-loving human beings.

"You the people have the power... the power to create happiness. You the people have the power to make this life free and beautiful, to make this life a wonderful adventure. Then in the name of democracy, let us use that power. Let us all unite! Let us fight for a new world, a decent world that will give men a chance to work, that will give youth a future, and old age a security."
~ Charlie Chaplin, from The Great Dictator, 1940

Wherever and whenever we see authoritarian regimes emerge throughout history, large segments of their populations are inevitably oppressed, brutalized and even murdered. These regimes completely ignore the One Idea. They will spew incessant propaganda to create the facade that they are virtuous, but the lie is apparent to anyone with a heart. They serve their own selfish state interests and have no sincere regard for the common good. As such, these sorts of regimes have no place in a healthy global community. They are doomed to fail and deservedly so.

RACISM

"Studies of the human genome have left absolutely no doubt that race is a fiction, that we're all cut from the same genetic cloth, that all of humanity is descended from a handful of people who walked out of Africa 55,000 years ago..."
~ Wade Davis, anthropologist[119]

Racism is a form of hatred directed toward those who are different. The idea of race, as Wade Davis points out, is a fiction. It is a lie. It only exists in our own minds. It is rooted in ignorance.

"Racism is not only socially divisive, but also scientifically incorrect. We are all descendants of people who lived in Africa recently. We are all Africans under the skin." ~ Spencer Wells[120]

Racism is totally opposed to the One Idea – that we are all one family, brothers and sisters. Racists cling to the false notion that we are separate. They refuse to acknowledge that they are connected to, and even descended from, other people of different skin color. Their egos demand that they be superior and that others be inferior. This is how they seek to justify their hatred of, and cruelty towards, others.

"No human race is superior; no religious faith is inferior. All collective judgments are wrong. Only racists make them."
~ Elie Wiesel, Nobel Laureate, Holocaust survivor[121]

I am not a skin color. I contain all of humanity in my heart and my mind, my flesh, my blood and my bones, and I am proud of that fact. You should be, too.

As a society and as individuals, we should denounce racial hatreds whenever and wherever they are exposed. Criminal acts of overt racism should be punished. We should also ensure that our laws promote equality for all people.

Again, parenting and education are key to eradicating racism once and for all. As parents and teachers, we have a responsibility to promote appreciation of other people and other cultures.

Our leaders, too, in all walks of life, must set a good example. We need to provide opportunities in our communities for people of all ethnic backgrounds to interrelate. Fear brings out the worst in people. Love brings out the best. When we get to know one another as people, as equals, our fears dissolve, our hatreds disappear. If you are a leader in your community in some capacity, ask yourself how you can further cultural understanding in your work.

THE ROLE OF INDIGENOUS PEOPLES

In talking about racism, it is important to take note of the suffering of indigenous peoples. The One Idea demands that all people be treated with dignity and respect.

Many different indigenous peoples around the world have been treated abominably by the dominant cultures that have supplanted them. There is a deep psychic wound in our collective consciousness. It is time for forgiveness and healing among all the colors and nations of the world.

A healthy future requires justice for all the indigenous peoples of the Earth. It is high time to address their grievances. There is no excuse for treating them as inferiors, for exploiting them and keeping them in circumstances of dire poverty. Speaking as an American, I am appalled at the continuing abusive treatment of Native Americans by the U.S. government. The abuse has been ongoing since Europeans first stepped foot on the continent.

We need to be honest about what has transpired in our history. Great travesties have been committed in the name of our government, our nation, and in the name of all the American people. In coming to terms with the sordid truth of our past, we can finally help to heal the wounds of our brothers and sisters of all ethnicities. Only then will we find our self-respect as a nation and be truly worthy of the respect of the rest of the world.

Indigenous peoples everywhere have much to teach us. We must give them opportunities to share their knowledge. They are the keepers of ancient wisdom that will serve the entire human family as we come together in harmony with Mother Earth to cope with the serious challenges ahead.

POVERTY AND THE POOR

"Verily I say unto you, inasmuch as ye have done it unto one of the least of these my brethren, ye have done it unto me."
~ Matthew 25:40

One of the most shameful developments taking place in American society is the orchestrated demonization of the poor for political gain.

By slandering the poor as no-good, lazy, low-lives undeserving of the expenditure of tax dollars, the 6's and 7's, in yet another shameless effort to increase their power and wealth, are deliberately appealing to the worst in people in order to win their votes and pass repressive and regressive legislation.

> *"In a country well governed, poverty is something to be ashamed of. In a country badly governed, wealth is something to be ashamed of."* ~ Confucius[122]

The poor can't afford to make campaign contributions. They have virtually no political power. What an easy target for the unconscionable bullies out there.

Every major religion and all people of good will recognize the importance of treating the poor and unfortunate in our society with kindness and generosity. When we have abundance, we must share. That's what the healthy human family is all about. We take care of one another. It is part of our social obligation and is directly related to the One Idea.

> *"He who oppresses the poor to increase his wealth and he who gives gifts to the rich – both come to poverty."* ~ Proverbs 22:16

> *"There is a key for everything, and the key to Paradise is love for the poor."* ~ The Prophet Muhammad[123]

> *"Speak up for those who cannot speak for themselves, for the rights of all who are destitute. Speak up and judge fairly; defend the rights of the poor and needy."* ~ Proverbs 31:8-9

> *"If a free society cannot help the many who are poor, it cannot save the few who are rich."* ~ John F. Kennedy[124]

Once again, this is all about the Golden Rule, isn't it? Treating others as you would like to be treated. Imagine if you were poor, if you were hungry, if you could see no way out of your circumstances. Is anyone there to help?

The Real Heroes are there – the 4's and 5's, who out of their love for humanity, stand up to defend the rights of the poor and the oppressed.

WOMEN'S RIGHTS

"I have faith in women and their potential. Women, by their very nature, bring people together. It is time for women to take the lead. We need to give them every opportunity to be educated and have the chance to act on what they know is best for all humanity." ~ Dr. Izzeldin Abuelaish, physician and author[125]

The One Idea demands justice for all. There can be no justice until women are respected and treated as equals.

Yet, the United Nations Development Fund for Women reports that at least one of every three women in the world will be beaten, raped or otherwise abused in her lifetime.[126]

In the workplace, women still don't even have equal pay with men![127]

Here in the 21st century, you would think we would know better. This is but another indication of the intensity of our collective spiritual illness.

No sex is better than or superior to another. Like yin and yang, male and female complement one another. Yet in too many places and in too many ways, women are victimized and treated in a subservient and demeaning fashion.

Women must be given every opportunity to flourish and to fulfill their highest potential as human beings. This is a very important part of realizing the One Idea and making this world a healthy place, where men and women work in harmony with mutual respect.

LGBT RIGHTS

"It matters not who you love, where you love, why you love, when you love or how you love, it matters only that you love."
~ John Lennon

Lesbian, gay, bisexual and transsexual people are entitled to the same rights as every other human being. We are One.

Sadly, even in the 21st century, there is still widespread ignorance regarding human sexuality. As with racism, this ignorance is rooted in fear of other people who are different.

Fear will always lead us down the wrong path. Courage, knowledge and wisdom will set us on the right path.

"Scientists from San Francisco to Stockholm are finding evidence of what gay people know in their hearts: that sexual orientation is innate. Recent research in Sweden has identified differences in brain structure that may determine whether a person is gay or straight." ~ James C. Hormel, U.S. Ambassador to Luxembourg[128]

Homosexuality is not a choice. Who would choose to be gay in a world that so often vilifies, mocks, brutalizes and ostracizes gay people? Nor is it a disorder.

"No, lesbian, gay, and bisexual orientations are not disorders. Research has found no inherent association between any of these sexual orientations and psychopathology. Both heterosexual behavior and homosexual behavior are normal aspects of human sexuality. Both have been documented in many different cultures and historical eras." ~ American Psychological Association[129]

Scientific studies are revealing that sexual orientation cannot be easily explained. Many factors appear to be involved including genetic, hormonal, developmental, social and cultural influences. Many scientists are of the opinion that both nature and nurture play complex roles.

"I believe all Americans who believe in freedom, tolerance, and human rights, have a responsibility to oppose bigotry and prejudice based on sexual orientation." ~ Coretta Scott King[130]

If you have any negative feelings toward LGBT people for being who they are, you need to explore your own heart and life experience for why this might be the case. The One Idea compels us to treat everyone with love, respect, and kindness.

THE BEAUTY OF THE RAINBOW

A rainbow is a beautiful thing. Take away any of its colors and it will be diminished.

Diversity, too, is a beautiful thing. The planet is diverse. The Universe is diverse.

"The diversity of the phenomena of nature is so great, and the treasures hidden in the heavens so rich, precisely in order that the human mind shall never be lacking in fresh nourishment."
~ Johannes Kepler, astronomer (1571-1630)[131]

As we move forward, our goal is not for all human beings to be the same. Equal in rights, yes, but we appreciate the beauty of our diversity.

"We all should know that diversity makes for a rich tapestry, and we must understand that all the threads of the tapestry are equal in value no matter what their color." ~ Maya Angelou

We have different languages, different foods, different ways of dress, different religions, different music. To have the privilege to encounter another culture is one of the most enriching experiences a human being can have. It is very important, therefore, to allow people to be who they are and allow them to express themselves freely.

Cultures and languages, like animal and plant species, are fast going extinct. Half of the languages in the world are not being taught to children and are disappearing forever.[132]

"When you lose a language, you lose a culture, intellectual wealth, a work of art. It's like dropping a bomb on the Louvre."
~ Kenneth L. Hale, linguist, MIT[133]

We must do our best to preserve different languages and cultures, because each difference offers new perspectives that help all of us to learn and grow.

What a dull, insufferable world this would be if we were all the same! If we all looked the same and acted the same and liked the same things and thought the same thoughts and believed the same things. Wait a minute. That sounds like what it's like to work for a corporation!

I'm only partly joking.

The power, reach, and influence of corporatism is sweeping across the globe. Corporatism doesn't care about who we are or what we feel or how we wish to live. Corporatism thrives on sameness. The giant multinationals want us all to behave and conform, so that we don't make waves or cause trouble or interfere with their Bottom Line which is always to make more and more money. In a corporate world, everything and everyone looks pretty much the same. No matter where you go, anywhere in the world, you can find the same boring corporate fast food joints and ugly big box stores.

The monolithic corporate world is stifling and oppressive. It is *not* about individual freedom. It is authoritarian in nature. It is devoid of art. It is devoid of heart. It is devoid of humanity.

Part of our shift in consciousness must be toward a renewed appreciation for not only human individuality, but for all that is beautiful in this world.

"Human beings have a consciousness by which we can appreciate love, beauty, creativity, and innovation or mourn the lack thereof... We can appreciate the delicacy of dew or a flower in bloom, water as it runs over the pebbles or the majesty of an elephant, the fragility of the butterfly or a field of wheat or leaves blowing in the wind. Such aesthetic responses are valid in their own right, and as reactions to the natural world they can inspire in us a sense of wonder and beauty that in turn encourages a sense of the divine." ~ Wangari Maathai, 2004 Nobel Peace Prize Laureate[134]

FOOD AND WATER ISSUES

"Water is a human right that should be kept out of the hands of profit-driven corporations." ~ Julia DeGraw, Food & Water Watch[135]

Those who are informed know that corporations are involved in a lot of nefarious activities, all in the name of increasing profits. Probably most horrifying is their ongoing attempt to control our food and water. Food and water are life itself.

It should come as no surprise that the corporate mainstream media aren't giving much attention to these issues at all. Powerful and entrenched business interests don't want there to be any public discussion. We have to look elsewhere for accurate information. I'm not going to go into all the issues surrounding food and water here, but again, I refer you to Appendix A to learn more.

For our own sakes, we all need to become aware of the food we are eating. We need to know where it comes from and how it is produced. The choices we make can have very negative consequences for our bodies and the environment.

We need to make positive, healthy choices for ourselves and for the planet. That's why many people are shopping for locally grown, organic foods. Others are growing their own herbs and vegetables. Some are buying their meat from small farmers and ranchers who treat their animals with respect. Many others are giving up meat altogether and becoming vegetarian or vegan for many of the same moral, ethical, and health reasons.[136] Yet, in American culture, these conscientious people are often mocked and made to feel like second-class citizens.

Food, like religion and politics, is a very personal issue. Every individual has specific dietary needs. We ought to respect everyone's personal choices. At the same time, we need to educate ourselves so that we can make the best choices for ourselves and our families. Parents, in particular, ought to make sure their kids are eating healthy foods.

Restaurants, schools, hospitals and other food providers have a responsibility to offer plenty of healthy food options to meet the dietary needs of all their customers and clients. Too many restaurants nowadays have very few options for vegetarians and almost none for vegans.

ANIMAL RIGHTS

"The greatness of a nation and its moral progress can be judged by the way its animals are treated." ~ Mahatma Gandhi

When we talk about food, we also must talk about animals and animal rights. Animals are being brutally abused in our factory farming systems. This is simply unacceptable, not to mention, unnecessary.

"If slaughterhouses had glass walls, everyone would be vegetarian." ~ Paul McCartney[137]

The corporate mainstream media won't pay any attention to this issue either, but there are many good films out there that are very informative (see Appendix A).

The One Idea embraces all, including animals. Animals are part of the whole. Anyone who doesn't love animals has a serious hole in the heart. Whenever a dog or a cat takes a liking to me, I know I must be doing something right.

"If any kid ever realized what was involved in factory farming, they would never touch meat again. I was so moved by the intelligence, sense of fun and personalities of the animals I worked with on 'Babe' that by the end of the film I was a vegetarian." ~ James Cromwell, actor[138]

If we are going to eat animals, use them for clothing, or for experimental purposes in our laboratories, it is incumbent upon our sense of decency that we minimize their pain and suffering, treat them with respect at all times, and honor the gifts that they provide to our bodies and our spirits.

"The more we learn of the true nature of non-human animals, especially those with complex brains and corresponding complex social behavior, the more ethical concerns are raised regarding their use in the service of man – whether this be in entertain-ment, as 'pets,' for food, in research laboratories, or any of the other uses to which we subject them." ~ Jane Goodall[139]

I am reminded of the Great Plains Native American tribes and their relationship to the buffalo, upon which they relied for their sustenance and way of life. At all times, they honored and respected the animal. They recognized their profound interrelationship in the greater scheme of things.

In fact, the Native American culture is very cognizant of the wisdom inherent in all the creatures in the animal kingdom. They know that each animal has much to teach us about ourselves, if only we take the time to observe, to reflect and to understand.

"If you talk to the animals they will talk with you and you will know each other. If you do not talk to them you will not know them and what you do not know you will fear. What one fears one destroys." ~ Chief Dan George

In many ways, our global shift in consciousness must be a shift back to the most ancient ways of knowing. The indigenous peoples, as I said, still carry this ancient knowledge and can teach us much, if we are willing to listen.

With the One Idea in mind, we recognize that the raising, feeding, care and slaughtering of the animals must always be done humanely and we must demand no less from the industries that provide our food, clothing, cosmetics, entertainment, etc.

Animals have just as much right to be on this planet as we do. We do not have the right, through our selfishness and our greed, to destroy their habitats and wipe them off the face of the Earth.

With every animal species that fades to extinction, one more opportunity is lost from the realm of human growth and possibility.

GATHERING TOGETHER

"Whatever we knew, whatever we learned, we shared, and by sharing we multiplied whatever courage we had individually."
~ Nelson Mandela[140]

The Real Heroes are gathering now. Are you ready to count yourself among them? They know that love represents all the best in life, that the pain and suffering of our brothers and sisters anywhere hurts us all. They are working to create a world that is fair and just. They stand up and speak out for what they believe when everyone else is silent.

"Each time a man stands up for an ideal, or acts to improve the lot of others, or strikes out against injustice, he sends forth a tiny ripple of hope and those ripples build a current which can sweep down the mightiest walls of oppression and resistance."
~ Robert F. Kennedy[141]

The Real Heroes work for peace. They understand the importance of the One Idea. They have accepted their responsibility to future generations. They are committed to caring for the Earth and all life upon it, and as we shall see in the next chapter, they are developing their Earth Consciousness.

CHAPTER SEVEN

Earth Consciousness

CHAPTER SEVEN

Earth Consciousness

"You should take care of your environment because the environment is you. You help create that environment, whether that is social environment or the natural environment."
~ Thich Nhat Hanh[142]

There it is again. The One Idea. Now that you are aware, you will begin to see it more and more in evidence all around you.

We are everything and everything is us. It's all One. What we do to others and the environment we do to ourselves.

We have a sacred trust to uphold. A trust that has been handed down from generation to generation. Respect is key to fulfilling our obligation. We must have respect, and teach respect, for Mother Earth and all living things.

To proceed wisely into the future, to aggressively put out those flames we've been talking about, we must develop our Earth Consciousness, on all levels – personal, social, business and institutional.

WHAT IS EARTH CONSCIOUSNESS?

Earth Consciousness, as I am going to use the term, is about having an awareness at all times of how our personal and communal actions, thoughts and feelings affect the Earth itself and all life upon it.

"A society grows great when old men plant trees in whose shade they know they shall never sit." ~ Greek Proverb

In previous chapters, I have discussed many ways in which our institutions, etc. have contributed to the flames of our burning house. Much of this negative behavior is the result of ignorance, selfishness and greed, all of which can be checked by asserting standards of basic human decency, which most of us, I do believe, still retain.

Earth Consciousness demands that we educate ourselves. Science is continually increasing our knowledge and understanding of the interconnectedness of all things, so we ought to pay attention to what the leading experts are telling us. Shame on the cutthroat corporations and their miscreant minions who are deliberately confusing the issues and disparaging what the scientists have to say, just so that they can continue to greedily leach dollar bills out of the exploitation and suffering of Mother Earth and her inhabitants.[143]

What is really required of all of us is a determination to care about one another, speak the truth, and do the right thing.

Earth Consciousness must become an ordinary part of our everyday lives. Every organization, every business, every school, every hospital, every institution, every government office ought to have people in management charged with the responsibility to pay close attention to green/sustainability issues and see that they are properly addressed. I believe that most of the changes that need to be made will be economically advantageous. It is in all of our best interests to think and be green.

> *"Nature is the infrastructure of our communities. If we want to leave a world that provides our children with opportunities for dignity and enrichment comparable to those we received, we must protect our environmental infrastructure – our air, water, fisheries, wildlife and the public lands that connect us to our past and give context to our communities that are the source of our values, virtues and character as a people."*
> ~ Robert F. Kennedy, Jr.[144]

Schools ought to be models for Earth Consciousness, making students aware of ongoing environmental issues. It's our children's future, after all, that is perilously at stake. They are the leaders of tomorrow and need to be prepared for what might lie ahead.

A NATIONAL INITIATIVE

America in times past has risen to some very serious challenges. Think of the mobilization of the entire country to gear up for World War II or the effort to put a man on the moon. We need a similar national initiative, led by concerned citizens of conscience, the U.S. government, the business sector, scientists, religious leaders and the media to make Earth Consciousness part of our everyday reality.

News media, especially, must step up to their social responsibilities and reclaim their rightful and necessary place as trustworthy truth tellers that serve the public interest.

Once the American public becomes informed and galvanized, then we can amass the forces and the wherewithal necessary to really take on these issues.

TAKING RESPONSIBILITY

Meanwhile, while we're waiting for the United States and the rest of the world's leaders to recover their sense of basic human decency and catch up with the moral imperative to do the right thing, the rest of us cannot be idle. We have a fire to put out and there is not a moment to lose.

Obviously, it is not possible to ever know exactly how everything we do, say, think and feel can affect others and the planet.

The more we understand the One Idea, how all of life is interconnected and interdependent, the more we can act in positive ways for the good of all.

As I said before, Earth Consciousness is something all of us need to make a part of our everyday reality. To give you an idea of what I'm talking about, I'm going to introduce you to Earth Conscious Frank. He's one of the number 4's, a good guy who is doing what he can to help put out the fire.

A DAY IN THE LIFE OF EARTH CONSCIOUS FRANK

The first thing Earth Conscious Frank does when he wakes up in the morning is to thank God, or his lucky stars, or whatever mystical configuration of chance and circumstance might be responsible for allowing him another day of life on this beautiful Earth. Frank recognizes his relation to the Universe and the humble, but important role he has to play within it. It is a gift for which he is grateful every day. He doesn't choose to waste it.

As Frank turns on the light in the bathroom, he notices that the light bulbs above the mirror aren't energy efficient. Frank is a guy who has become conscious of the three R's: Reduce, Reuse, Recycle. He makes a mental note that he needs to replace those bulbs for more eco-friendly ones.

In the shower, Frank uses a minimal amount of non-toxic shampoo, knowing that the less he consumes, the better it is for the planet. He ends the shower as soon as he's finished rinsing, so as not to waste water unnecessarily.

When Frank brushes his teeth, he uses a minimal amount of toothpaste and turns on the water only for the brief time he actually needs it.

As Frank gets dressed, he takes satisfaction in knowing that most of the clothes he has were purchased at a second-hand store that donates its proceeds to a charity he really likes. He smiles to think that others might pay $50 for a trendy, designer-label shirt, but the one he puts on only cost him five bucks – and it looks great, too!

Frank has a healthy breakfast: whole grain toast, fresh-squeezed orange juice and steel-cut oatmeal with blueberries. Frank is particularly mindful of what he eats. He avoids processed foods and tries to buy local and organic when he can. He became vegetarian several years ago for a variety of reasons including his concern for the welfare of factory farm animals and the environment. He says he's lost weight and feels great.

Frank is a consumer like the rest of us, but he doesn't buy a bunch of stuff that he doesn't need, stuff that lasts a short while and ends up in a landfill. He tries to support local businesses as much as possible in all his purchases. He works hard for the money he makes and doesn't like to spend it on companies that he can't support in good conscience – companies that don't respect the environment, their customers or their employees.

Unfortunately, Frank doesn't have access to convenient public transportation and his job is many miles away, so a bicycle just doesn't work for him. He's not happy about it, but he does what he can to save energy. He traded in his gas-guzzler for a compact car that gets comparatively good mileage. When driving in town, he turns off the ignition if he has to wait more than 10 seconds at a light. He does the same when waiting to fill his tank. Frank knows that even these small acts are good for the planet, his conscience, and his wallet.

When Frank is on the freeway, he drives no more than 60 mph to save fuel. He's been doing it for several years now. He knows he goes slower than almost everyone else, of course, but he finds he is more relaxed while driving and no longer in a hurry to reach his destination. He really enjoys the ride!

Frank works for a B corporation that is socially and environmentally conscious. It's a company that is doing good things for the community. He receives a fair wage and enjoys the work.

On the way home, he stops to pick up some cash. He recently switched all his banking to a credit union and he is very glad he did. The credit union provides him with better, more personal service than the Big Banks, higher interest rates on his savings account and lower fees. Frank says he feels much better knowing the credit union is owned and operated by its members who are part of his community and working for its benefit.

Frank is constantly on the lookout for more ways to lessen his own environmental "footprint." He always finds time to read articles, books, and blogs to educate himself about issues of concern, and every day he advocates for the better world he believes in. He frequently signs petitions and writes letters/emails to his government representatives. Recently, he participated in a march to support women's rights.

Frank has wonderful loving relationships with his family. He spends as much quality time as possible with them. He and his wife share the workload around the house. She works, too, and has a very satisfying career. Frank makes it a point to be involved with his children's education. He helps them with their homework every evening and makes sure they communicate often about how things are going at school.

Frank leads a simple life, but he's very happy. He has good, positive relationships with his family, his work, and even the Earth itself. On the weekends, the whole family enjoys working on their backyard garden together. They grow fresh herbs and vegetables, as well as flowers. Often, they take outings to get back to nature, picnicking in the parks, hiking in the mountains, or kayaking in the nearby lakes and rivers.

If you ask Frank how much he has sacrificed to be Earth Conscious, he would tell you he hasn't sacrificed at all. None of the changes he has made have been difficult and every choice has made his life better in some way. His lifestyle is healthier, less stressful, more affordable, and much more meaningful. He feels better about himself and the world.

These are just a few of the sorts of choices Frank makes everyday. You, of course, will make your own choices, given what's important to you. The Internet is an invaluable resource to find not only information, but also other people who are taking positive steps to promote change.

"At times our own light goes out and is rekindled by a spark from another person. Each of us has cause to think with deep gratitude of those who have lighted the flame within us."
~ Albert Schweitzer

Isn't it gratifying to know that we are all in this together, doing what we can to make this world a better place? When we take action, we inspire one another. In the next and final chapter, we're going to go one step further. We're going to dare to imagine the new world we are creating together.

CHAPTER EIGHT

A Vision for a New World

CHAPTER EIGHT

A Vision for a New World

"Another world is not only possible, she is on her way. On a quiet day, I can hear her breathing." ~ Arundhati Roy, novelist[145]

Well, dear reader, you made it with me to the final chapter of this book. Congratulations! Many gave this book the old heave-ho into the wastebasket pages ago! Truth has always been painful to hear. Denial is so much more comfortable.

You know, however, that only by confronting the truth can we summon the wisdom necessary to deal with the compelling issues that face us all. That's why you've stayed with me, even though you may have disagreed with me here and there along the way. We all have our own perceptions, based on our knowledge and experience. None of us will ever agree entirely.

But I hope we can all agree on the importance of love. Love is what all of this is about. Love for one another, for our planet, and all life upon it.

ANOTHER WORLD IS POSSIBLE

Throughout this book, we have seen how the institutions that we have created – our government, our media, our corporations, our health care system, our financial systems, etc. – are not abiding by the Golden Rule; they are not treating us the way we deserve to be treated. Money has taken precedence over the needs of human beings, the planet, and our fellow creatures.

Greed, selfishness, and mean-spirited behavior on all levels of our society have supplanted basic human decency. We have turned away from love and courage to embrace hatred and fear.

No wonder we have gone horribly astray and our house, our earthly home, is burning. We need to grow up. We need to become responsible adults who recognize that we are all in this together. Every one of us needs to do everything he/she can to help put out the fire.

The One Idea shows us the way to a better, healthier world. That is our objective after all, to create a healthy world that meets our basic needs. It is an idea that all of us must make part of our everyday awareness. As we do, we will find our immediate external worlds changing, the conflicts in each of our lives will find amicable resolutions and the greater external world itself will begin to heal, becoming less fearful, less violent, more contented and more peaceful.

It really is not difficult to achieve. It is as simple as the truth of the Golden Rule. All it requires is an act of will on the part of each of us. We must commit to compassion and live a compassionate life.

IMAGINE ALL THE PEOPLE...

Now, let's take a few moments to imagine the better world that awaits us if only we have the courage and the will to realize it.

Remember, everything that is made physical in our human experience first begins with an idea. A chair can't be created without someone first conceiving an idea of what that chair might look like. Our new world cannot be created without our own clear vision of what we would like it to be.

Throw away any old conventional box that is limiting your imagination. Don't be afraid to be idealistic or unrealistic. We need idealists in this world, the dreamers who inspire us to realize our potential. We will always be striving for an ideal in any endeavor; that's how progress is made. The ideal shows us the way.

"A dream you dream alone is only a dream, but a dream you dream together is reality." ~ Yoko Ono[146]

If we applied the One Idea as I'm suggesting in this book, our world would change significantly. It is a world in which most people of all "races" and creeds get along, work well together, and treat one another with respect. (Remember that race is an illusion – that's why I put it in quotes.)

So here we go. Let's envision our new world...

There are still many different religions and cultures and ways of seeing and experiencing, but people celebrate their diversity and learn from the thinking and ideas of others.

"Rivers, lakes, ponds, streams, oceans, all have different names, but they all contain water. So do religions have different names, and they all contain truth..." ~ Muhammad Ali[147]

Only the most unbalanced people believe in hate and fear anymore. Love and courage have become the order of the day.

Science, too, is valued and respected for providing knowledge and insight into the mysterious ways of the Universe. Everyone knows that advances in science and technology are key to solving many of the most difficult problems that face humankind, but those advances are being tempered with wisdom, taking into account the interrelationship of all things.

People are very open-minded. They can entertain divergent points of view without becoming upset or hostile. They value truth and honesty in their personal lives and they demand it from their institutions. It is amazing that the news media, which used to be such a divisive force for political pandering and slandering, have restored the traditional standards of journalistic integrity to their operations. People are well informed about what's happening in the world.

The job situation has changed dramatically. The shift to a green economy created an exciting boom in the job market as new technologies, products and services were developed. Most people love going to work, because their talents are suited to their jobs. Employers have evolved in their attitudes toward their employees, treating them with the respect they deserve. Wages are fair, job conditions are safe, and benefits are generous. In return, the employees are very loyal and committed to making their companies successful, knowing that their jobs are vital to their own security, well-being, and self-esteem.

Corporations, too, have evolved so that their primary reason for being is to serve the public good in some way. Profits are still important, but greed is no longer what makes the corporations tick. Consequently, the corporate pollution and exploitation of the planet that used to be so commonplace has virtually ceased, except for the few rogue exceptions. Most refreshingly, the stifling, authoritarian corporate environment and culture has given way to a real sense of what can only be described as "creative fun and adventure." Of course, this is all due to an enlightened and compassionate management style that takes into account the needs of the employees.

The people at the top have changed, too. CEO's and other executives, acting out of good faith and good conscience, no longer accept outrageous pay and unconscionable bonuses and many have even become highly respected members of their communities!

As for the government, it's lean and efficient and completely democratic. All over the world great changes have been taking place since these democratic governments have been responding to the needs of the people they serve. In the U.S., those ideals where everyone is "created equal" with "liberty and justice for all" are finally being realized.

Much of the waste has been eliminated from politics. Remember all that time and money that used to be spent in the circus atmosphere of those silly elections? The people said, "No more," and took all that money out of politics and channeled it where it belongs, into more important things like health care, schools, bridges and roads.

In fact, in our new world, all people have access to quality education and affordable health care. The literacy rate of the entire world has increased dramatically. The poor, the sick, and the elderly are properly cared for. All that brutal business where insurance companies fleeced the patients or denied them care has ended! No one has to fear becoming destitute because of old age or disease anymore. Imagine all the stress that has been removed from people's lives. That fact alone has made them healthier.

Every city has plenty of green spaces, public parks and recreation facilities for all to enjoy. You see people exercising all the time. They are more physically healthy than they have ever been. Of course, that's one reason runaway health care costs came under control. People weren't getting sick like they did before. Pharmaceuticals also lost their appeal as people realized they weren't doing what they were supposed to do. Some drugs were causing even more problems and making people more sick. Nowadays, people know that medicine has its place, but diet and nutrition, mental health, and exercise are what people need most to stay healthy. Preventing illness has become as important as treating it.

In this dream we dream together, everyone is taken care of. Everyone's basic survival needs have been met. Food is healthy. Water is clean.

Education has been improved, too. Higher education is now widely available and affordable. Teachers are highly regarded in their communities.

As literacy has increased, poverty, crime and violence have declined. Many neighborhoods, just like in the old days, are so safe that people leave their homes without locking the doors. And that makes perfect sense, doesn't it? When people's basic needs are met, they no longer become desperate and feel the need to commit crimes.

The overall quality of life has increased dramatically, even though the planet is still undergoing severe challenges in climate change. Life is still very difficult in that regard. That's unfortunate, but understandable, given the fact that humanity took so long to wake up and get its act together.

Still, in our new world, we all know that we can rely on one another. We have strong communities based on love and respect. Whatever challenges we face, we meet them head on.

In the olden days, the planet itself was disrespected, the oceans were very nearly killed off completely, but now everyone values their relationship to the Earth and works together to prevent abuse and exploitation. Habitats, too, are protected so that wildlife can thrive. We've seen too many animals go extinct due to human arrogance and thoughtlessness – the polar bear, the tiger, the mountain gorilla – and we can't allow that to continue. Resources are conserved and used wisely. In fact, thanks to our educational efforts, people are so Earth Conscious, one rarely sees litter of any kind anymore.

The energy needs of the planet, which had been so daunting for so long, have finally been met with scientific ingenuity. New technologies make use of renewable resources: solar, wind, hydrogen, biomass, geothermal, etc. These advances are incorporated in all new building designs and modes of transportation. It's remarkable to see how far we've come, once we put our minds to it.

Thankfully, the Earth is now returning to balance and harmony once again. We have reconnected with nature. The whole of planet Earth is becoming healthier day by day.

Perhaps most importantly we now have wise, democratically elected leaders making decisions around the world, leaders who are truly concerned about the citizens they serve, rather than their own egos and bank accounts. Idiotic, costly wars and despotic rulers have become a thing of the past. People work together through cooperative diplomatic channels to resolve conflicts.

It is very interesting that the militarization of the planet that was so threatening to freedom and democracy became totally unnecessary once the fear mongering stopped and the greedy, war-machine opportunists lost their power and influence.

Peace and a kind of non-materialistic prosperity have become widespread. Many now find ample time to spend with their families and their loved ones. Many are engaged in creative pursuits that bring out the best in themselves and lead to very fulfilling lives.

Imagine that!

Peace on Earth. Goodwill to all.

Can such words become more than an insincere banality uttered once a year? Is this dream world we envision really so far-fetched? Close your eyes for a moment and try to feel what it would be like. Take a breath of its fresh, clean air. It's not called socialism or communism or capitalism or any of those other -isms people use to divide us from one another. It's called sanity.

NO ROSE-COLORED GLASSES ALLOWED

Unfortunately, a dream is just a dream. We always have to wake up. We have to assess our world realistically and make our best choices accordingly. Rejoin us now in our present-day world of insanity.

It's hard to wake up, isn't it?

Okay. Realistically speaking, how much of our dream world can we actually achieve? Frankly, much of it is indeed possible. No, we will never have perfect people living in complete harmony, but still, we have to admit that we collectively created the world we see now and we have the ability to re-create it along much healthier lines if we choose. It is not, however, at this point in time, very likely that we will.

Even so, that doesn't mean it is not worth working and fighting for. Perhaps through our efforts today it will seem much more likely tomorrow.

We have to take sides in the conflict between good and "evil." The real evil as I said is within us, not without. The evil is our own selfishness, greed, hate, arrogance, cruelty, and indifference.

"Hate is not the opposite of love; apathy is." ~ Rollo May[148]

There are too many who have given in to the worst in themselves and allowed that to be okay, as if somehow it doesn't really matter. It does matter. To all of us. We are interconnected.

BECOMING OUR BEST SELVES

"The worst sin towards our fellow creatures is not to hate them, but to be indifferent to them: that's the essence of inhumanity."
~ George Bernard Shaw[149]

Being good or being evil is not something that is inherent in our nature over which we have no control, rather we define ourselves by the choices we make, moment by moment, situation by situation. All it takes is an act of will to be the best that we can be.

"The evolutionary instinct compels us to bring out the best in ourselves and in others, to recognize our interconnectedness with everyone else." ~ Jonas Salk[150]

Our real challenge is to become the people who care, the people who love, the people who act on behalf of all. We need to become the 4's and the 5's who do everything they can to put out the fire. When you commit to being your best, your personal world will change dramatically, even if the greater external world continues on its disheartening suicidal path. That alone is worth the effort.

"Any time you have an opportunity to make a difference in this world and you don't, then you are wasting your time on Earth."
~ Roberto Clemente[151]

There are way too many 1's, 2's and 3's in the world right now who are ignorant, scared, unwilling to help, or just don't care. Meanwhile, the 6's and 7's, the most lamentable of human beings, go on in their merry way pretty much running – and destroying – the world.

HOPE

Where does our hope lie? Our hope lies in the essential goodness of human beings.

Wade in the Wave

Every stone I cast
on water ripples

to the edge of an unknown
world

and when in time
another stone skims past

the hand I know not
rippling why

remembers
the choosing of the rock

its color and touch
immortal, divine.

Our hope lies in our finally recognizing the truth of the One Idea. Love and compassion have the power to redeem and save us.

"When you love, you wish to do things for. You wish to sacrifice for. You wish to serve." ~ Ernest Hemingway[152]

Our individual power to effect change may not seem like much, but remember, we are all interconnected: We are One. Powerlessness itself is an illusion. The truth is that the tiny bucket we each carry is capable of achieving great deeds. We are all part of a whole. Every positive action we take, no matter how small, will have an impact.

"Remember there's no such thing as a small act of kindness. Every act creates a ripple with no logical end." ~ Scott Adams[153]

THE END AND THE BEGINNING

"How wonderful it is that nobody need wait a single moment before beginning to improve the world." ~ Anne Frank[154]

So here we are at last at the end of the book. I have my bucket. You have yours.

The fire may be raging, but we both know there are many, many 4's and 5's out there who are already pitching in and even more are on the way. They come from all over the world, from all walks of life and from every religion. They believe in the One Idea, too, even if they don't know it.

They believe in all of us – working together. They believe we will rise to the challenge.

They believe in the best of humanity, not the worst.

They are good people and they give us all hope.

And you, dear reader.

You give us all hope, too.

Appendices

APPENDIX A

References and Resources

PRINT

Abuelaish, Izzeldin. *I Shall Not Hate: A Gaza Doctor's Journey on the Road to Peace and Human Dignity*, Random House, Canada, 2010.

Armstrong, Karen. *Twelve Steps to a Compassionate Life*, Alfred A. Knopf, NY and Canada, 2010.

Bartlett, Bruce. *Impostor: How George W. Bush Bankrupted America And Betrayed The Reagan Legacy*, Doubleday, NY, 2006.

Begley, Ed, Jr. *Ed Begley, Jr.'s Guide to Sustainable Living: Learning to Conserve Resources and Manage an Eco-Conscious Life*, Clarkson Potter, 2009.

Benn, Hilary. "Biodiversity nears 'point of no return,'" BBC News, bbc.co.uk, Jan. 17, 2010.

Ben-Shahar, Tal. *Happier: Learn the Secrets to Daily Joy and Lasting Fulfillment*, McGraw-Hill, 2007.

Brzezinski, Zbigniew. *Out of Control: Global Turmoil on the Eve of the 21st Century*, Touchstone, NY, 1995.

Carter, Jimmy. *Our Endangered Values: America's Moral Crisis*, Simon & Schuster, NY, 2005.

Chomsky, Noam. *Profit Over People: Neoliberalism & Global Order*, Seven Stories Press, NY, 2011.

Chopra, Deepak. *Ageless Body, Timeless Mind*, Three Rivers Press, 1993.

Clements, Jeffrey D. *Corporations Are Not People: Why They Have More Rights Than You Do and What You Can Do About It*, Berrett-Koehler Publishers, 2012.

Cohn, Jonathan. *Sick: The Untold Story of America's Health Care Crisis – and the People Who Pay the Price*, Harper, 2007.

Coll, Robert. *Private Empire: ExxonMobil and American Power*, Penguin Press HC, 2012.

Cortright, David. *Peace: A History of Movements and Ideas*, Cambridge University Press, 2008.

Davis, Wade. *The Wayfinders: Why Ancient Wisdom Matters in the Modern World*, House of Anansi Press, Toronto, Canada, 2009.

Ehrlich, Paul R. and Anne H. Ehrlich. *Betrayal of Science and Reason: How Anti-Environmental Rhetoric Threatens Our Future*, Island Press, 1998.

Ehrlich, Paul R. and Robert E. Ornstein, *Humanity on a Tightrope: Thoughts on Empathy, Family, and Big Changes for a Viable Future*, Rowman & Littlefield, 2010.

Einstein, Albert. *The World As I See It*, Open Road Integrated Media, NY, 2011.

Eisler, Riane. *The Chalice and the Blade*, Harper Collins Publishers, Inc., NY, 1987.

Eisler, Riane. *The Real Wealth of Nations*, Berrett-Koehler Publishers, San Francisco, CA, 2008.

Frank, Anne. *The Diary of a Young Girl*, Everyman's Library, reprint edition, 2010.

Frankl, Viktor E. *Man's Search for Meaning*, Beacon Press, Boston, MA, 2006.

Fromm, Erich. *The Art of Loving*, Harper Perennial Modern Classics, 2006.

Fuller, Richard Buckminster. *And It Came To Pass Not To Stay*, MacMillan Publishing Co., NY, 1976.

Gandhi, Mahatma and Louis Fischer, ed. *The Essential Gandhi: An Anthology of His Writings on His Life, Work and Ideas*, Vintage Spiritual Classics, NY, 1962.

Gandhi, Mahatma and Thomas Merton, ed. *Gandhi on Non-Violence*, New Directions, 2007.

Gerhards, Paul. *Mapping the Dharma: A Concise Guide to the Middle Way of the Buddha*, Parami Press, Vancouver, WA, 2007.

Goleman, Daniel. *Emotional Intelligence*, Bantam Books, 2006.

Goodall, Jane. *Hope for Animals and Their World: How Endangered Species Are Being Rescued from the Brink*, Grand Central Publishing, NY, 2009.

Goodell, Jeff. "As the World Burns: How Big Oil and Big Coal mounted one of the most aggressive lobbying campaigns in history to block progress on global warming," Rolling Stone, rollingstone.com, Jan. 6, 2010.

Greenwald, Glenn. *With Liberty and Justice For Some: How the Law Is Used to Destroy Equality and Protect the Powerful*, Metropolitan Books, 2011.

Hacker, Jacob S. and Paul Pierson. *Winner-Take-All Politics: How Washington Made the Rich Richer—and Turned Its Back on the Middle Class*, Simon & Schuster, NY, 2010.

Hall, Kevin G. "Why haven't any Wall Street tycoons been sent to the slammer?" McClatchy Newspapers, mcclatchydc.com, Sep. 20, 2009.

Hanh, Thich Nhat. *Love In Action: Writings on Non-Violent Social Change*, Parallax Press, Berkeley, CA, 1993.

Hansen, James. "Game Over for the Climate," The New York Times, May 9, 2012.

Hartmann, Thom. *The Last Hours of Ancient Sunlight: The Fate of the World and What We Can Do Before It's Too Late*, Three Rivers Press, 1998.

Hartmann, Thom. *Threshold*, Viking Penguin, 2009.

Hawken, Paul. *The Ecology of Commerce Revised Edition: A Declaration of Sustainability*, HarperBusiness, 2010.

Hawking, Stephen. *A Brief History of Time*, Bantam Books, NY, 1998.

Hedges, Chris. *Empire of Illusion: The End of Literacy and The Triumph of Spectacle*, Nation Books, NY, 2010.

Hoggan, James. *Climate Cover-Up: The Crusade to Deny Global Warming*, Greystone Books, D&M Publishers Inc., Vancouver, Canada, 2009.

Hormel, James C. and Erin Martin. *Fit to Serve: Reflections on a Secret Life, Private Struggle, and Public Battle to Become the First Openly Gay U.S. Ambassador*, Skyhorse Publishing, 2011.

Kahlenberg, Richard D. and Moshe Z. Marvit. "A Civil Right to Unionize," The New York Times, Feb. 29, 2012.

Kaku, Michio. *Physics of the Future: How Science Will Shape Human Destiny and our Daily Lives by the Year 2100*, Doubleday, 2011.

Kapur, Sahil. "GOP to investigate 'scientific fraud' of global warming: report," The Raw Story, Nov. 3, 2010.

King, Martin Luther Jr. and James M. Washington, ed. *A Testament of Hope: The Essential Writings and Speeches of Martin Luther King, Jr.*, HarperOne, NY, 1990.

Kirby, David. *Animal Factory: The Looming Threat of Industrial Pig, Dairy, and Poultry Farms to Humans and the Environment*, St. Martin's Press, 2010.

Klein, Naomi. *The Shock Doctrine: The Rise of Disaster Capitalism*, Picador, NY, 2008.

Krauss, Lawrence. *A Universe from Nothing: Why There is Something Rather than Nothing*, Free Press, 2012.

Kristof, Nicholas D. "Our Banana Republic," The New York Times, Nov. 6, 2010.

Krugman, Paul. "Betraying the Planet," The New York Times, Jun. 28, 2009.

Kumar, K. Raghul. "On Big Bang Singularity Dynamics," Millennium Relativity, mrelativity.net, Jan. 11, 2010.

Kushner, Lawrence. *I'm God, You're Not: Observations on Organized Religion & Other Disguises of the Ego*, Jewish Lights Publishing, Woodstock, VT, 2010.

Lakoff, George. *The Political Mind: A Cognitive Scientist's Guide to Your Brain and Its Politics*, Penguin, 2009.

Lappé, Anna. *Diet For A Hot Planet*, Bloomsbury, NY, 2010.

Lazonick, William. "How American Corporations Transformed From Producers to Predators," AlterNet, alternet.com, Apr. 1, 2012.

Ledbetter, James. *Unwarranted Influence: Dwight D. Eisenhower and the Military-Industrial Complex*, Yale University Press, New Haven & London, 2011.

Loeb, Paul. *Soul of a Citizen: Living with Conviction in Challenging Times*, St. Martin's Press, NY, 2010.

Loewen, James W. *Lies My Teacher Told Me: Everything Your American History Textbook Got Wrong*, Touchstone, 2007.

Lundin, John with His Holiness The Dalai Lama. *The New Mandela: Eastern Wisdom for Western Living*, Helix Publishing, 2010.

Madrick, Jeff. *Age of Greed: The Triumph of Finance and the Decline of America, 1970 to the Present*, Alfred A. Knopf, 2011.

Mandela, Nelson. *Long Walk to Freedom: The Autobiography of Nelson Mandela*, Back Bay Books, 1995.

Maslow, Abraham. *Toward a Psychology of Being*, Van Nostrand Reinhold Co., NY, 1968.

Mayer, Jane. *The Dark Side: The Inside Story of How The War on Terror Turned Into a War on American Ideals*, Doubleday, 2008.

McKibben, Bill. *Deep Economy: The Wealth of Communities and the Durable Future*, Times Books, NY, 2007.

McKibben, Bill. *Eaarth: Making a Life on a Tough New Planet*, Times Books, NY, 2010.

McKibben, Bill. *The End of Nature*, Random House, NY, 1989.

McKie, Robin. "Attacks paid for by big business are 'driving science into a dark era,'" The Guardian, UK, Feb. 18, 2012.

Mehl-Madrona, Lewis. *Coyote Medicine: Lessons From Native American Healing*, Fireside, 1997.

Merton, Thomas. *The Seven Storey Mountain*, Mariner Books, 1999.

Mokhiber, Russell. *Corporate Crime and Violence: Big Business Power and the Abuse of the Public Trust,* Random House, 1989.

Moore, Kathleen Dean and Michael P. Nelson. *Moral Ground: Ethical Action for a Planet in Peril,* Trinity University Press, 2010.

Moyers, Bill. *Moyers on Democracy,* Doubleday, 2008.

Neihardt, John G. *Black Elk Speaks: Being the Life Story of a Holy Oglala Sioux,* University of Nebraska Press, 1988.

Oreskes, Naomi and Erik Conway. *Merchants of Doubt: How a Handful of Scientists Obscured the Truth on Issues from Tobacco Smoking to Global Warming,* Bloomsbury Press, NY, 2010

Palmer, Chris. *Shooting in the Wild: An Insider's Account of Making Movies in the Animal Kingdom,* Sierra Club Books, 2010.

Peck, M. Scott. *The Road Less Traveled: A New Psychology of Love, Traditional Values and Spiritual Growth,* Simon & Schuster, 1978.

Pollan, Michael. *In Defense of Food: An Eater's Manifesto,* Penguin Press, 2007.

Pollan, Michael. *The Omnivore's Dilemma: A Natural History of Four Meals,* Penguin Press, 2006.

Potter, Wendell. *Deadly Spin: An Insurance Company Insider Speaks Out on How Corporate PR is Killing Health Care and Deceiving Americans,* Bloomsbury Press, NY, 2010.

Rees, Martin. *Our Final Hour,* Basic Books, NY, 2003.

Ruiz, Don Miguel. *The Four Agreements Toltec Wisdom Collection,* Amber-Allen Publishing, 2008.

Scahill, Jeremy. *Blackwater: The Rise of the World's Most Powerful Mercenary Army,* Nation Books, 2007.

Schopenhauer, Arthur. *On the Basis of Morality,* Hackett Publishing Co., Indianapolis/Cambridge, 1998.

Schweiger, Larry J. *Last Chance: Preserving Life on Earth,* Fulton Publishing, Golden, CO, 2009.

Schweitzer, Albert. *Out of My Life and Thought: An Autobiography,* The Johns Hopkins University Press, Baltimore, MD, 2009.

Sharlet, Jeff. *C Street: The Fundamentalist Threat to American Democracy,* Little, Brown and Company, 2010.

Simon, Stephanie. "The Secret to Turning Consumers Green," The Wall Street Journal, online.wsj.com, Oct. 18, 2010.

Sirota, David. *Back to Our Future: How the 1980s Explain the World We Live In Now,* Ballantine Books, 2011.

Stiglitz, Joseph. "Foreclosures and banks' debt to society: Rewritten bankruptcy provisions reduce indebted homeowners to servitude. What has become of the rule of law in the US?" The Guardian, guardian.co.uk, Nov. 5, 2010.

Stockdale, Charles B., Michael B. Sauter, and Douglas A. McIntyre, "The Ten Biggest American Cities That Are Running Out Of Water," 24/7 Wall St., Nov. 1, 2010.

Suzuki, David and Dave Robert Taylor. *The Big Picture: Reflections on Science, Humanity, and a Quickly Changing Planet,* published by Greystone Books in partnership with the David Suzuki Foundation, Vancouver, Canada, 2009.

Suzuki, David, with Amanda McConnell & Adrienne Mason. *The Sacred Balance: Rediscovering Our Place in Nature,* Greystone Books in partnership with the David Suzuki Foundation, Vancouver, Canada, 2007.

Taibbi, Matt. *Griftopia: Bubble Machines, Vampire Squids, and the Long Con That Is Breaking America,* Spiegel & Grau, NY, 2010.
Thoreau, Henry David. *Civil Disobedience and Other Political Writings,* American Renaissance Books, 2009.
Thoreau, Henry David. *Walden; or, Life in the Woods,* Dover Publications, 1995.
Toffler, Alvin. *Future Shock,* Random House Publishing Group, NY, 1984.
Trenberth, Kevin, Sc.D. "Check with Climate Scientists for Views on Climate," Wall Street Journal, Feb. 1, 2012.
Tutu, Desmond. *God Has a Dream: A Vision of Hope for Our Time,* Doubleday, 2004.
Tyson, Neil Degrasse, and Donald Goldsmith. *Origins: Fourteen Billion Years of Cosmic Evolution,* W. W. Norton, NY, 2005.
Vidal, John. "Protect nature for world economic security, warns UN biodiversity chief," The Guardian, UK, Aug. 16, 2010.
Washington Post editorial. "Climate change denial becomes harder to justify," The Washington Post, May 15, 2011.
Wells, Spencer. *Deep Ancestry: Inside the Genographic Project,* National Geographic, 2007.
Wells, Spencer. *Pandora's Seed: The Unforeseen Cost of Civilization,* Random House, NY, 2010.
Wiesel, Elie. *Night,* Bantam Books, NY, 1982.
Williams, Mary Elizabeth. "When bullies go to work: The hidden epidemic of workplace mistreatment affects over a third of workers – and is hurting us all," salon.com, Mar. 7, 2012.
Wright, Ronald. *A Short History of Progress,* Carroll & Graf, NY, 2004.

FILM & VIDEO

The 11th Hour, a film by Leonardo DiCaprio, 2007.
The Age of Stupid, a film by Franny Armstrong, 2009.
An Inconvenient Truth, a film by Davis Guggenheim, 2006.
Beyond Our Differences, a film by Peter Bisanz, aired on Bill Moyers Journal, PBS, 2008.
The Big Fix, a film by Josh and Rebecca Tickell, 2011.
Bill Moyers Journal, Moyers' interview with author John Nichols and constitutional scholar Bruce Fein, PBS, Jul. 13, 2007.
Blue Gold: World Water Wars, a film by Sam Bozzo, 2008.
Capitalism: A Love Story, a film by Michael Moore, 2009.
The Corporation, a film by Mark Achbar and Jennifer Abbott, 2003.
The Cove, a film by Louie Psihoyos, 2009. Won Academy Award for Best Documentary Feature, 2010.
Crude: The Real Price of Oil, a film by Joe Berlinger, 2011.
A Crude Awakening: The Oil Crash, a film by Basil Gelpke and Ray McCormack, 2006.
David Versus Monsanto, a film by Bertram Verhag, 1999.
Deep Green, a film by Matt Briggs, 2010.
Dirt, a film by Bill Benenson and Gene Rosow, 2009.
Earth 2100, a TV program presented by ABC, 2009.

Earthlings, a film by Shaun Monson, 2005.
The Elegant Universe, Peabody Award-winning miniseries with physicist Brian Greene, PBS, 2011.
The End Of The Line, a film by Rupert Murray, 2009.
Fair Game, a film by Doug Liman, 2010.
Farm to Fridge: The Truth Behind Meat Production, a video by Lee Iovino, 2011.
Fast Food Nation, a film by Richard Linklater and Eric Schlosser, 2006.
Flow: For Love Of Water, a film by Irena Salena and Steven Starr, 2008.
Food, Inc., a film by Robert Kenner and Eric Schlosser, 2008.
Forks Over Knives, a film by Lee Fulkerson, 2011.
Fresh, a film by Ana Sofia Joanes, 2009.
Fuel, a film by Josh Tickell, 2008.
The Future of Food, a film by Deborah Koons, 2004.
Gasland, a film by Josh Fox, 2010.
Green, a film by Patrick Rouxel, 2009.
Home, a film by Yann Arthus-Bertrand, 2009.
Inside Job, a film by Charles H. Ferguson, 2010.
Joseph Campbell and The Power of Myth, Bill Moyers, PBS series, 1988.
King Corn, a film by Ian Cheney and Curt Ellis, 2007.
Koch Brothers Exposed, a film by Robert Greenwald, 2012.
Mclibel, a film by Franny Armstrong and Ken Loach, 2005.
Money, Power & Wall St., Frontline, aired on PBS, Apr. 24 and May 1, 2012.
The Last Mountain, a film by Bill Haney, 2011.
No Impact Man, a film by Laura Gabbert and Justin Schein starring Colin Beavan, 2009.
Origins: Fourteen Billion Years of Cosmic Evolution, hosted by astrophysicist Neil deGrasse Tyson, Nova, PBS, 2004.
Orwell Rolls in his Grave, a film by Robert Kane Pappas, 2003.
Outfoxed: Rupert Murdoch's War on Journalism, a film by Robert Greenwald, 2004.
Processed People: The Documentary, a film by Jeff Nelson, 2009.
The Real Dirt on Farmer John, a film by Taggart Siegel, 2005.
Sicko, a film by Michael Moore, 2007.
The Story of Citizens United v. FEC, a video by Annie Leonard, 2011.
The Story of Stuff, a video by Annie Leonard, 2007.
Supersize Me, a film by Morgan Spurlock, 2004.
Wal-Mart: The High Cost of Low Price, a film by Robert Greenwald, 2005.
What's On Your Plate, a film by Catherine Gund, 2009.
Who Killed the Electric Car? a film by Chris Paine, 2006.
Why We Fight, a film by Eugene Jarecki, 2005.
Wonders of the Universe, a video series with physicist Brian Cox, The Science Channel, 2011.
World Peace and Other 4th Grade Achievements, a film by Chris Farina, 2010.
The World According To Monsanto, a film by Marie-Monique Robin, 2008.
The Yes Men Fix the World, a film by Andy Bichlbaum and Mike Bonanno, 2009.

APPENDIX B

The Charter for Compassion

As we move forward, for all of our sakes, we need to commit to being caring human beings. Kindness and compassion must become part of our everyday lives.

I hope you will join me in affirming the Charter for Compassion. You can learn more about the Charter and sign on at charterforcompassion.org.

According to the Charter's website, *"The Charter for Compassion is a document that transcends religious, ideological, and national differences. Supported by leading thinkers from many traditions, the Charter activates the Golden Rule around the world."*

The Charter for Compassion, which was unveiled in 2009, states:

> **The principle of compassion** *lies at the heart of all religious, ethical and spiritual traditions, calling us always to treat all others as we wish to be treated ourselves. Compassion impels us to work tirelessly to alleviate the suffering of our fellow creatures, to dethrone ourselves from the centre of our world and put another there, and to honour the inviolable sanctity of every single human being, treating everybody, without exception, with absolute justice, equity and respect.*

> **It is also necessary** *in both public and private life to refrain consistently and empathically from inflicting pain. To act or speak violently out of spite, chauvinism, or self-interest, to impoverish, exploit or deny basic rights to anybody, and to incite hatred by denigrating others—even our enemies—is a denial of our common humanity. We acknowledge that we have failed to live compassionately and that some have even increased the sum of human misery in the name of religion.*

> **We therefore call upon all men and women** *~ to restore compassion to the centre of morality and religion ~ to return to the ancient principle that any interpretation of scripture that breeds violence, hatred or disdain is illegitimate ~ to ensure that youth are given accurate and respectful information about other*

traditions, religions and cultures ~ to encourage a positive appreciation of cultural and religious diversity ~ to cultivate an informed empathy with the suffering of all human beings—even those regarded as enemies.

We urgently need *to make compassion a clear, luminous and dynamic force in our polarized world. Rooted in a principled determination to transcend selfishness, compassion can break down political, dogmatic, ideological and religious boundaries. Born of our deep interdependence, compassion is essential to human relationships and to a fulfilled humanity. It is the path to enlightenment, and indispensible to the creation of a just economy and a peaceful global community.*

By affirming the charter, we acknowledge the importance of compassionate behavior in our world. Over 88,000 people have affirmed so far. Won't you join us?

Acknowledgements

Given the interconnectedness of life, one can be influenced in so many ways by the actions, ideas, and comments of others. Some of these influences are made conscious; many others are not. This book was, in part, inspired by a coffee-shop conversation in Portland, Oregon, with Rev. Robert L. Schaibly who, in his younger days, marched for civil rights with Rev. Dr. Martin Luther King, Jr. Bob and I talked about how the world was on fire, but few were paying attention, and fewer still were doing anything about it in their daily lives. It occurred to me then that there might be a book in there somewhere circulating around this notion. Considerable thought, reading, life experience and reflection followed for a number of years before I finally put pen to paper and finger to keyboard.

My thanks to Rev. Schaibly and all those thoughtful, compassionate human beings, especially the writers, artists, poets, musicians, environmentalists, scientists, ministers, healers and truth seekers, who continually engage the serious issues of the world in search of practical remedies to the pain and suffering that continually confront and obstruct our peaceful passage on this planet. Many of them are quoted in this book. They inspire me daily to continue my own work in this regard.

I want to thank also those who took the time to read this book in its pre-publication draft form, make comments in support of it, relate their personal responses to the material, offer their strong encouragement and even occasionally correct a typo or two.

My biggest thanks, of course, is reserved for my loving and staunchly supportive wife Nancy McDonald, without whom this book would only be a mirage, never materializing into a finished form worthy of public consideration. That fateful day I met her changed my life forever. I am eternally grateful for the synchronistic alignment of space and time that threaded its way into the Great Mystery of this Universe and finally brought us together.

**Many thanks to the following for their permissions
that came with such kindness and good wishes:**

Dr. Izzeldin Abuelaish, Madeleine Austin and World Business Academy,
Peter Bisanz, Stephen Eric Bronner, Raffi Cavoukian, Julia DeGraw,
Riane Eisler, Thom Hartmann, Paul Hawken, Arianna Huffington,
Lawrence Krauss, Rabbi Lawrence Kushner, Peter Lehner,
Paul Rogat Loeb, Yoko Ono, Rosalie Sorrels, David Suzuki, Jodi Tatum
and the Charter for Compassion Team, Neil deGrasse Tyson, and
Writers House as agent for The Heirs to the Estate of Martin Luther
King Jr.

List of Poems

ALL POEMS BY LAURENCE OVERMIRE

The following poems were previously published:

Less Than Infinity (earlier version); Fiber; Big Fish, Small Pond; Techno Man; and Real World appear in *Report From X-Star 10,* Laurence Overmire, Indelible Mark Publishing, 2009.

Good Guys and Bad Guys first published in Commonsense 2, Aug. 2008.

The Honorable Intention first published in *Taj Mahal Review*, Dec. 2006.

Forgiveness first published in Badosa Poetry Library, June 2003.

Wade in the Wave appeared in *World's Strand Anthology*, 2006.

Notes

CHAPTER ONE: THE HOUSE IS ON FIRE

[1] Anne Frank, *The Diary of a Young Girl*, Bantam [Paperback], 1997, page 333.
[2] Thomas Lewis, Fari Amini, and Richard Lannon, *A General Theory of Love*, Random House, NY, 2000, p. 219.
[3] Archbishop Desmond Tutu, from an interview in *Beyond Our Differences*, a film by Peter Bisanz, aired on Bill Moyers Journal, PBS, 2008.
[4] Stephen Eric Bronner, "At Home With the Bigot," Reader Supported News, Feb. 14, 2012. Bronner is Director of Global Relations at the Center for the Study of Genocide, Conflict Resolution, and Human Rights, Rutgers University.

CHAPTER TWO: SOUNDING THE ALARM

[5] Stephen Hawking interviewed by Elizabeth Vargas, "Changes in Our Solar System: Is Trouble Coming?" 20/20, ABC News, abcnews.go.com, Aug. 16, 2006. Hawking also warns that climate change could have a disastrous effect on rainforests, in the Amazon and elsewhere, which have been described as the lungs of the planet. He emphasizes the urgent need to reverse global warming if indeed it is still possible.
[6] Raffi Cavoukian, "The Right to a Future: Urgent need for a new lens and lexicon for conveying climate collapse," Centre for Child Honouring, childhonouring.org, Jan. 2011.
[7] Union of Concerned Scientists, "Global Warming Science," ucsusa.org, Feb. 2012.
[8] World Business Academy, "The True Story About 'Climate Cover-Up: The Crusade to Deny Global Warming,'" Truthout, Dec. 9, 2009.
[9] Martin Rees, *Our Final Hour*, Basic Books, NY, 2003, p. 8.
[10] National Geographic News, "Big-Fish Stocks Fall 90 Percent Since 1950, Study Says," May 15, 2003.
[11] World Wildlife Fund, "As Few as 3,200 Tigers Left," 2011.
[12] Kevin Trenberth, Sc.D, Distinguished Senior Scientist, Climate Analysis Section, National Center for Atmospheric Research, "Check with Climate Scientists for Views on Climate," Wall Street Journal, Feb. 1, 2012. Also see statements on climate change from 18 scientific associations, "Scientific Consensus on Global Warming," Union of Concerned Scientists, ucsusa.org.
[13] Peter Lehner, "The Media, Climate Science, and Deniers: Time to Tell a New Story," Natural Resources Defense Council, switchboard.nrdc.org, Sep. 7, 2010.
[14] "Global Environment Outlook: environment for development (GEO-4)," United Nations Environmental Programme, Box 5.3, p.162, 2006. See also "The Pleistocene-Holocene Event: The Sixth Great Extinction," The Rewilding Institute, rewilding.org, from *Rewilding North America*, by Dave Foreman, Island Press, WA, 2004.

[15] "The State of the Planet's Biodiversity: Key Findings from the Millennium Ecosystem Assessment," United Nations Environmental Programme, June 5, 2010. The Living Planet Report 2012, published by the World Wildlife Fund, reveals that since 1970 biodiversity across the planet has declined by about 30% (60% in the tropics).

[16] For a list of Endangered Species (includes 10,801 endangered animals and 9322 endangered plants) see "Worldwide Endangered Animal List," Earth's Endangered Creatures, earthsendangered.com, May 21, 2010.

[17] As I write this, the inhabitants of the Pacific island nation of Kiribati are making plans to flee their homes. "Entire nation of Kiribati to be relocated over rising sea level threat," by Paul Chapman, Wellington, The Telegraph, UK, Mar. 10, 2012.

[18] Michio Kaku, *Physics of the Future: How Science Will Shape Human Destiny and our Daily Lives by the Year 2100,* Doubleday, 2011, p. 222.

CHAPTER THREE: THE ONE IDEA

[19] William Shakespeare, *Hamlet,* Act III, Scene I.

[20] Neil deGrasse Tyson, *The Universe: The Complete Season 1,* History Channel, Nov. 20, 2007.

[21] John Muir, *My First Summer in the Sierra,* Houghton Mifflin, Boston, MA, 1911.

[22] Vaughns Summaries, World Population Growth Table, updated Feb. 18, 2012.

[23] Spencer Wells, *Spencer Wells builds a family tree for humanity,* Ted Talks, ted.com, Jun. 2007.

[24] Albert Einstein, from a letter written February 12, 1950.

[25] Martin Luther King, Jr., *Remaining Awake Through a Great Revolution,* Commencement Address for Oberlin College, Oberlin, OH, Jun. 1965.

[26] Erich Fromm, *The Art of Loving,* Harper, 1956.

[27] Black Elk, *The Sacred Pipe: Black Elk's Account of the Seven Rites of the Oglala Sioux,* recorded and edited by Joseph Epes Brown, University of Oklahoma Press, 1953.

[28] Viktor Frankl, *Man's Search For Meaning,* Pocket Books, a division of Simon & Schuster Inc., New York, NY, 1984, p. 57.

[29] Thomas Merton, final address at a conference on East-West monastic dialogue, Dec. 10, 1968. He died 2 hours later.

[30] Webster's New Universal Unabridged Dictionary, Deluxe Edition Revised and Updated, Random House, 1996.

[31] Karen Armstrong, "9/11 and Compassion: We Need it Now More Than Ever," Huffington Post, Sep. 10, 2010.

[32] See various websites including: "The Universality of the Golden Rule in the World Religions," teachingvalues.com; "Shared Belief in the Golden Rule," Ontario Consultants on Religious Tolerance, religioustolerance.org; "World Scripture: the Golden Rule," unification.net; "Golden Rule and the Global Ethic," Scarboro Missions, scarboromissions.ca; "The Golden Rule Poster," Interfaith Unity, interfaithunity.ca; "Universality of the Golden Rule," Edmonton Interfaith Centre for Education and Action, edminterfaithcentre.ca; "World Religious

Texts," truthbook.com; "The Golden Rule," Wikipedia, wikipedia.org; "The Golden Rule," Humanity Healing International, humanityhealing.org; "Golden Rule," about.com; "Islamic Resources," futureofchildren.net; "Classic Wisdom: The Golden Rule," ye-gods.info; "The Golden Rule," Universal House of Justice, uhj.net; "The Golden Rule – The Ethic of Reciprocity," foodforthesoul.hubpages.com.

[33] Lawrence Krauss, *A Universe From Nothing,* a film by Josh Timonen, produced by The Richard Dawkins Foundation for Reason and Science, 2009.

CHAPTER FOUR: THE WORLD AT SIXES AND SEVENS

[34] I recognize the word "American" can refer to anyone living on the North or South American continents. For the sake of convenience, when I use the word "American" in this book, I am referring to the United States.

[35] John Adams, Letter to J. H. Tiffany, Mar. 31, 1819.

[36] Voltaire, *Questions sur les miracles,* 1765.

[37] Dwight D. Eisenhower, Address Recorded for the Republican Lincoln Day Dinners, Jan. 28, 1954.

[38] From the notes of Dr. James McHenry, one of Maryland's delegates to the Convention, first published in *The American Historical Review,* vol. 11, 1906, p. 618.

[39] Henry David Thoreau, *Walden; or, Life in the Woods,* Ticknor and Fields, 1854.

[40] "Facts on Media in America: Did You Know?" Common Cause, commoncause.org, Feb. 20, 2012

[41] William Shakespeare, *Macbeth,* Act V, Scene V.

[42] Quoted from an interview with Bill Moyers, "David Stockman on Crony Capitalism," Moyers & Company, Jan. 21, 2012.

[43] Dwight D. Eisenhower, Address on the Farm Bill Veto, April 16, 1956.

[44] See, for example, constitutional scholar Bruce Fein's interview with Bill Moyers in which he talks about the undermining of Congressional authority, the erosion of checks and balances, and the assumption of extraordinary powers by the George W. Bush administration. Bill Moyers Journal, PBS, Jul. 13, 2007.

[45] Benjamin Franklin, *An Historical Review of the Constitution and Government of Pennsylvania,* published by Benjamin Franklin, 1759.

[46] Mark Twain, draft manuscript (c.1881), quoted by Albert Bigelow Paine in *Mark Twain: A Biography,* 1912.

[47] Alex Blumberg, "Senator By Day, Telemarketer By Night," Planet Money, npr.org, Mar. 30, 2012. Sen. Dick Durbin laments how much time a senator must spend thinking about, talking about, and planning for various means of raising money.

[48] Martin Luther King, Jr. *Letter from Birmingham Jail,* Apr. 16, 1963.

[49] Quoted in *Wisconsin: A History,* by Robert C. Nesbit, The University of Wisconsin Press, p. 384.

[50] Theodore Roosevelt, *The Progressive Covenant With The People,* Aug. 1912.

[51] Theodore Roosevelt, *The New Nationalism,* address at Osawatomie, Kansas, Aug. 31, 1910.

[52] Thom Hartmann, The Daily Take, RT News, Nov. 4, 2011.

[53] Edmund Pellegrino, M.D., "one of the deans of modern medical ethics," quoted in "What Would Jesus Do?" Tides & Currents, americantidesandcurrents.com, 2012.

[54] In fact, health insurance companies have a financial incentive to deny health care to patients. The less care the insurance company actually provides, the more money it makes.

[55] Caldwell Esselstyn, Jr., M.D., interviewed in the film *Processed People: The Documentary,* directed by Jeff Nelson, 2009.

[56] Riane Eisler, *The Real Wealth of Nations,* Berrett-Koehler Publishers, San Francisco, CA, 2008, p. 157-8.

[57] Ibid, p. 131.

[58] John Steinbeck, *Once There Was a War,* 1958.

[59] General Omar Bradley, Armistice Day speech Nov. 11, 1948, *Collected Writings, Volume 1,* 1967.

[60] Franklin writing to a friend a week after the Treaty of Paris was signed in 1783.

[61] John Dalberg-Acton, Letter to Mandell Creighton, Apr. 5, 1887.

[62] Quoted in "Bishop Tutu: It's Time To Make Compassion Fashionable," by Ed and Deb Shapiro, Huffington Post, Sep. 14, 2010.

[63] Lincoln's First Inaugural Address, Mar. 4, 1861.

CHAPTER FIVE: DOUSING THE FLAMES

[64] Karen Armstrong, from an interview in *Beyond Our Differences,* a film by Peter Bisanz, 2008.

[65] William Shakespeare, *As You Like It,* Act 5, Scene 1.

[66] Joseph Campbell, *The Power of Myth,* an interview with Bill Moyers, PBS, 1988.

[67] Lawrence Kushner, *I'm God, You're Not: Observations on Organized Religion & Other Disguises of the Ego,* Jewish Lights Publishing, Woodstock, VT, 2010, p. 122.

[68] Jung, C.G., revised and edited by Aniela Jaffe, *Memories, Dreams, Reflections,* Pantheon Books, New York, 1962.

[69] Paine, Thomas, *Rights of Man. Part the Second. Combining Principle and Practice,* 1792.

[70] Quoted from a 1981 speech in *A Documentary History of the United States,* by Richard D. Heffner, New American Library, 2002, p. 479.

[71] Ronald Reagan, Speech to Temple Hillel and Community Leaders in Valley Stream, Oct. 26, 1984, jewishvirtuallibrary.org.

[72] Rutherford B. Hayes, *The Life, Public Services and Select Speeches of Rutherford B. Hayes,* by James Quay Howard, Robert Clarke & Co., Cincinnati, OH, 1876, p. 253.

[73] Bill Moyers, *Our Politicians Are Money-Launderers in the Trafficking of Power and Policy,* speech for Public Citizen 40th Gala, Washington, D.C., Oct. 20, 2011.

[74] Paul Rogat Loeb, "Soul of a Citizen: What Cynicism Costs Us," paulloeb.org.

75 Albert Einstein, Tribute to Pablo Casals, Mar. 30, 1953, in *Conversations with Casals* by Josep Maria Corredor, 1957.

76 Clarence Darrow, *Argument of Clarence Darrow in the case of the Communist Labor Party in the Criminal Court, Chicago*, C. H. Kerr, 1920.

77 Deepak Chopra, *The Deeper Wound: Recovering the Soul from Fear and Suffering*, Harmony Books, 2001.

78 Martin Luther King, Jr., "An Experiment in Love," *Jubilee*, September 1958, pp. 11ff.

79 David Montgomery, "Flowers, Guns and an Iconic Snapshot," The Washington Post, Mar. 18, 2007.

80 Martin Luther King, Jr. Accepting Nobel Peace Prize, Dec. 10, 1964.

81 David Suzuki & Dave Robert Taylor, *The Big Picture: Reflections on Science, Humanity, and a Quickly Changing Planet*, , published by Greystone Books in partnership with the David Suzuki Foundation, 2009, p. 204. Reprinted with permission from the publisher.

82 Quoted in News Journal, Mansfield, Ohio, Aug. 3, 1965.

83 Ambrose Bierce, *The Devil's Dictionary*, Neale Publishing Co., 1911.

84 Richard D. Kahlenberg and Moshe Z. Marvit, "A Civil Right to Unionize," The New York Times, Feb. 29, 2012. The authors credit organized labor with helping to build the middle class in the U.S. and helping to pass key legislation like Medicare and the Civil Rights Act. They also emphasize that the 1948 Declaration of Human Rights acknowledged the right of people to form unions to protect their interests.

85 William Shakespeare, *Hamlet*, Act 1, Scene 5.

86 BCorporation.net, 2012.

87 Paul Hawken, *The Ecology of Commerce: A Declaration of Sustainability*, HarperCollins Publishers, Inc., New York, NY, 1993.

88 Dwight D. Eisenhower, *The Chance for Peace*, speech to the American Society of Newspaper Editors, Washington, D.C., Apr. 16, 1953.

89 Martin Luther King Jr., *Beyond Vietnam: A Time to Break Silence*, address at Riverside Church, New York City, Apr. 4, 1967.

90 See Keir A. Lieber and Robert J. Lieber, "The Bush National Security Strategy," U.S. Foreign Policy Agenda, U.S. Department of State, Dec. 2002.

91 The Third and Fourth Geneva Conventions established that prisoners would not be tortured in armed conflicts. The United Nations Convention Against Torture also prohibited torture and has been ratified by 147 countries as of September 2010. Wikipedia, 2012. See also "The Geneva Conventions of 1949 and Their Additional Protocols," International Committee of the Red Cross, icrc.org.

92 George Washington, *The Writings of George Washington, Vol. XII, 1790-1794*, G.P. Putnam's Sons, 1891, p.452.

CHAPTER SIX: THE REAL HEROES

93 Leo Tolstoy, "Three Methods Of Reform" in *Pamphlets: Translated from the Russian*, 1900, as translated by Aylmer Maude, p. 29.

[94] Robert Walsh, "Life of Benjamin Franklin," *Delaplaine's Repository of the Lives and Portraits of Distinguished Americans* (Philadelphia, 1815-17), II, 51-2.

[95] Thomas Jefferson to Thomas Jefferson Smith, February 21, 1825. A transcription of the original letter is available from the University of Virginia. Original manuscript in the Library of Congress: Thomas Jefferson Papers.

[96] Quote from *The Two Towers* (2002), screenplay by Fran Walsh, Philippa Boyens, Stephen Sinclair, and Peter Jackson, the second part of Peter Jackson's *The Lord of the Rings*, New Line Cinema, based on the J.R.R. Tolkien trilogy.

[97] Lao Tzu, *Tao Te Ching*, c. 6th century BCE.

[98] Martin Luther King, Jr. *Beyond Vietnam: A Time to Break Silence.*

[99] Mother Teresa, *Where There is Love, There is God,* Doubleday, 2010.

[100] What came before the Big Bang is still a profound mystery. As Michio Kaku notes, a singularity is a "point of infinite gravity from which nothing can escape." Even light cannot escape. Therefore it is "a horizon beyond which we cannot see." Michio Kaku, *Physics of the Future,* p. 101.

[101] Webster's, p. 1547.

[102] Bukkyo Dendo Kyokai, *The Teaching of Buddha,* BDK America, bdkamerica.org.

[103] Walt Whitman, preface to *Leaves of Grass,* Brooklyn, NY, 1855.

[104] Matthew 5:39; Luke 6:29.

[105] Quoted in "JC Penney CEO: 'Ellen Represents The Values Of Our Company,'" by Zack Ford, Think Progress LGBT, thinkprogress.org, Feb. 9, 2012.

[106] Rainer Maria Rilke, *Letters to a Young Poet*, Letter Seven, May 14, 1904.

[107] Reinhold Niebuhr, *The Irony of American History*, Charles Scribner's Sons, 1952.

[108] Leonard Cohen, from his song *Anthem.*

[109] Congressional Record – Senate, Vol 153, Pt. 16, July 31, 2007, p. 21573.

[110] P. D. James, *Time to Be in Earnest: A Fragment of Autobiography,* Ballantine Books, 1999.

[111] Quoted in "'Travelin' Lady' Rosalie Sorrels," by Jean Sheldon, ezinearticles.com, Sep. 3, 2011

[112] Johann Wolfgang von Goethe, *Maxims and Reflections,* translated by Bailey Saunders, The MacMillan Company, 1906.

[113] See, for example: "'Texas schoolbook massacre' rewrites American history," by Guy Adams, The Independent, UK, Mar. 28, 2010.

[114] *The Adams Papers Digital Edition,* ed. C. James Taylor, Charlottesville: University of Virginia Press, Rotunda, 2008. Original Source: Legal Papers of John Adams, Volume 3, Cases 63 and 64.

[115] The Organization for Economic Co-operation and Development (OECD) ranked the U.S. 14th in the world for reading, math, and science in 2010: Jessica Shepherd, "World education rankings: which country does best at reading, math, and science?" Guardian, UK, Dec. 7, 2010.

[116] Catherine Rampell, "Teacher Pay Around the World," The New York Times, Mar. 18, 2012. See also "Education at a Glance, 2009: OECD Indicators," oecd.org.

[117] Robert Maynard Hutchins, *The University of Utopia,* University of Chicago Press, 1953.

[118] James Madison, letter to W. T. Barry, Aug. 4, 1822.

[119] Wade Davis, TED Talks, TEDxWhistler, Feb. 18, 2010.

[120] Spencer Wells, *The Rediff Interview/Dr Spencer Wells,* rediff.com, Nov. 27, 2002.

[121] Elie Wiesel, "Have You Learned The Most Important Lesson Of All?" Parade Magazine, May 24, 1992.

[122] Analects of Confucius, Chapter VIII, ca. 475 - 221 BCE.

[123] As reported by Ibn Umar, Al-Hadis, 1:280, quoted in "The Hadiths," inaedadrieasda.net.

[124] John F. Kennedy, Inaugural Address, Jan. 20, 1961.

[125] Izzeldin Abuelaish, *I Shall Not Hate: A Gaza Doctor's Journey on the Road to Peace and Human Dignity,* Random House, Canada, 2010.

[126] "Get the Facts," International Violence Against Women Act, passivawa.org.

[127] Amanda Hess, "Women Make Less Than Men at Every Education Level," Good News, www.good.is, Feb. 29, 2012.

[128] James Hormel, "Being gay is not a choice," Special to CNN, cnn.com, Nov. 16, 2011.

[129] American Psychological Association, apa.org.

[130] Quoted in "The Sexual Continuum," by Dr. Brian Mustanski, *Psychology Today,* Jan. 17, 2011.

[131] Johannes Kepler, *Mysterium Cosmographicum,* Tübingen, 1596.

[132] Wade Davis, *The Wayfinders: Why Ancient Wisdom Matters in the Modern World,* House of Anansi Press, Toronto, Canada, 2009, p. 3.

[133] Ibid, p. 5.

[134] Wangari Maathai, *Replenishing the Earth: Spiritual Values for Healing Ourselves and the World,* Doubleday, 2010.

[135] Julia DeGraw, Food & Water Watch, a consumer advocacy organization that works to ensure clean water and safe food, foodandwaterwatch.org, May 21, 2011.

[136] There are many reasons why people are choosing to eat less meat or become vegetarian. Here are a few: 1) To help fight poverty and hunger. It takes about 7 pounds of grain to grow 1 pound of beef. Therefore, about 7 times more humans could be fed without needing additional land. 2) To lower the carbon footprint. A United Nations report noted that eating meat causes almost forty per cent more carbon emissions than all the cars, trucks, ships and planes in the world combined. 3) To reduce pollution. Meat production produces enormous amounts of manure that end up polluting rivers and streams. 4) To improve health. There are a wide variety of health benefits to eating vegetarian or vegan, from lowering blood pressure and cholesterol to preventing obesity and diabetes. 5) To show respect for animals. Factory farm practices are often brutally abusive to animals. 6) To prevent deforestation. As Thom Hartmann notes on p. 46 of *Last Hours of Ancient Sunlight,* "72 acres of rainforest are destroyed every minute, mostly by impoverished people working for

multinational corporations, who are cutting and burning the forest to create agricultural or pasturelands to grow beef for export to the United States. This 38 million acre loss per year will wipe out the entire world's rainforests in our children's lifetimes."

[137] Sir Paul McCartney, *Glass Walls,* a film by PETA, peta.org.

[138] Quoted in "Celebrities For Animals," Earth Angels Animal Sanctuary, earthangelsanimalsanctuary.org.

[139] Jane Goodall, *Through a Window: My Thirty Years with the Chimpanzees of Gombe,* Mariner Books, 2000, p. 245.

[140] Nelson Mandela, *Long Walk to Freedom: The Autobiography of Nelson Mandela,* Back Bay Books, 1995.

[141] Robert F. Kennedy, *Day of Affirmation Address,* University of Capetown, South Africa, Jun. 6, 1966.

CHAPTER SEVEN: EARTH CONSCIOUSNESS

[142] Thich Nhat Hanh, "The Environment is You: A Talk by Thich Nhat Hanh, Denver, Colorado, August 29, 2007," Human Architecture, Journal of the Sociology of Self-Knowledge, Vol. 6, Iss. 3, 2008.

[143] As NASA climate scientist Dr. James E. Hansen contends in "The Real Deal: Usufruct & the Gorilla," Columbia.edu, 2007, the intent of those who are deceiving the public about climate change is to create confusion and thereby delay any effective action on the issue. He warns that the delay could "cause tipping points to be passed" leading to the loss of Arctic sea ice, for example, rising sea levels and great loss of plant and animal species.

[144] Robert F. Kennedy, Jr., robertfkennedyjr.com.

CHAPTER EIGHT: A VISION FOR A NEW WORLD

[145] Arundhati Roy, *Confronting Empire,* closing speech at the World Social Forum, Porto Allegre, Brazil, Jan. 27, 2003.

[146] Yoko Ono, Imagine Peace, imaginepeace.com.

[147] Muhammad Ali, *The Soul of a Butterfly: Reflections on Life's Journey,* Simon & Schuster, 2004.

[148] Rollo May, *Love and Will,* W.W. Norton & Company, 1969.

[149] George Bernard Shaw, *The Devil's Disciple,* 1901.

[150] Quoted in *On Becoming Fearless: in Love, Work, and Life,* by Arianna Huffington, Little, Brown, and Company, 2006.

[151] Quoted in "He just can't kick the baseball habit," by Peter Leo, *Pittsburgh Post-Gazette,* Jul. 11, 2006.

[152] Ernest Hemingway, *A Farewell to Arms,* 1929.

[153] Scott Adams, "A Kind Word," a letter to Scott Adams' Internet fans, Newsletter #9, Dec. 1995.

[154] Anne Frank, *The Diary of a Young Girl.*

Index

ABOUT THE AUTHOR

Laurence Overmire has had a multi-faceted career as poet, author, actor, director, educator, and genealogist. As an actor, he has appeared on stage, film and television, most notably on Broadway in *Amadeus*, as well as the network soap operas, *All My Children* and *Loving*. His award-winning poetry has been widely published in hundreds of journals, magazines and anthologies worldwide. Known to many for his weekly segments as poet-in-residence on The Jeff Farias Show, Overmire is an advocate for peace, justice, human and animal rights, and the environment.

WANT TO HELP FIGHT THE FIRE?

Join the Bucket Brigade at:

www.TheOneIdeaThatSavesTheWorld.com

www.facebook.com/TheOneIdeaThatSavesTheWorld

$\frac{5}{14}$
123

$\frac{6}{4}$

CPSIA information can be obtained at www.ICGtesting.com
Printed in the USA
BVOW040622010313

314370BV00001B/2/P